MW01448993

PERFECT

MATCH

PERFECT

BABOLAT AND TENNIS SINCE 1875

PREFACES
BJÖRN BORG
RAFAEL NADAL
TEXTS
CHARLOTTE GABAS

ABRAMS | NEW YORK

BABOLAT ADDIXION

ROLAND GARROS
Babolat

ROLAND
GARROS
Babolat

PREFACES

ABOVE Björn Borg presents La Coupe des Mousquetaires (The Musketeers' Cup) to Rafael Nadal following his victory against Novak Djokovic on 8 June 2014.

Babolat has become one of the leading brands in the world of tennis and, most importantly for me, it played a major part in my career. Over the course of many years, I relied on its natural gut strings – they were vital to my life as a professional tennis player, and I think it's fair to say that I did pretty well in that department! In my day, the whole world was adamant it wanted to play with the VS string as it was the gold standard, a guarantee of quality. What I like very much about Babolat is that it is first and foremost one big family servicing the needs of its players. Its teams were always there for me, every step of the way from the beginning of my career to the very end. If I needed a string or even racquets strung in a hurry, wherever I was in the world, there was always someone on hand to help me. The racquets, the strings and all the teams that work within the company are incredible. I've had the opportunity to visit the factory in Lyon on several occasions and I've been blown away by the professionalism and expertise prevailing there. At Babolat, they know what they're doing. I feel very honoured and happy, therefore, to have been part of this great family, along with Rafa Nadal, Carlos Alcaraz and so many other players who have opted for the best equipment there is. Thank you Babolat and a happy 150th birthday!

— Björn Borg

How could anyone select just a single anecdote from this extraordinary story? For me, however, there is one that probably best sums up Babolat's flexibility and dedication during my career.

In 2022, I decided to alter the weight of my racquet for the hardcourt season. This paid off very quickly, as I won the Australian Open, followed by a tournament in Acapulco. But as the clay court season approached, I began to have doubts, since I did not know if I would be able to control my "spin" or the speed of the ball on that surface. Unfortunately, I injured myself in the final at Indian Wells, which disrupted my preparations for playing on clay. I returned to Madrid, but injured my foot again in Rome, one week before Roland–Garros. I was running out of time, so I made the decision to train, using the new racquet. However, on the night before the tournament, I changed my mind as I realised I would not be able to control the ball properly. So, I called Jean–Christophe at Babolat and said to him: "Look, I can't win Roland–Garros with this racquet, I've got to go back to my old one." They had just one day to organise everything, which meant returning to Lyon and getting the racquets ready. The teams managed to get them to me a few hours before the start of the tournament and the warm–up and I sensed I'd made the right decision. The rest is history as between us we won Roland–Garros!

In conclusion, Babolat and I have enjoyed a very close relationship since I was very young. I can remember my first Soft Drive, the Pure Drive and then the first time I set eyes on the Aero Pro, the racquet I used most in my career. On that day, Babolat had come to see me with a completely different frame from the one I was used to. It felt strange at first but, as soon as I tried it out, I loved it. And ultimately, it became the racquet of my life!

Thank you to the Babolat family for all the help you gave me and the confidence you always showed in me over the course of so many years!

— Rafael Nadal

CONTENTS

BABOLAT

DESTINED FOR TENNIS

1875

1900

THERE ARE DESTINES DEPENDENT ON VERY LITTLE AND EPIC JOURNEYS DRIVEN BY THE AUDACITY OF AN IDEA. SOMETIMES THERE ARE SEEMINGLY INNOCUOUS ENCOUNTERS THAT CAN TOTALLY CHANGE EVERYTHING AND LEAD TO CERTAIN HISTORIES BECOMING INTERTWINED. THAT'S PRETTY MUCH HOW IT WAS WITH TENNIS AND BABOLAT, TWO WORLDS THAT MIGHT NEVER HAVE MET, UNTIL ONE DAY IN 1875, A CHANCE MEETING LED TO THE WISH TO TAKE A GAMBLE WITH THE RESULT THAT TWO DISPARATE PATHS JOINED TOGETHER TO EMBARK ON THE CRAZIEST OF FAMILY AND ENTREPRENEURIAL ADVENTURES.

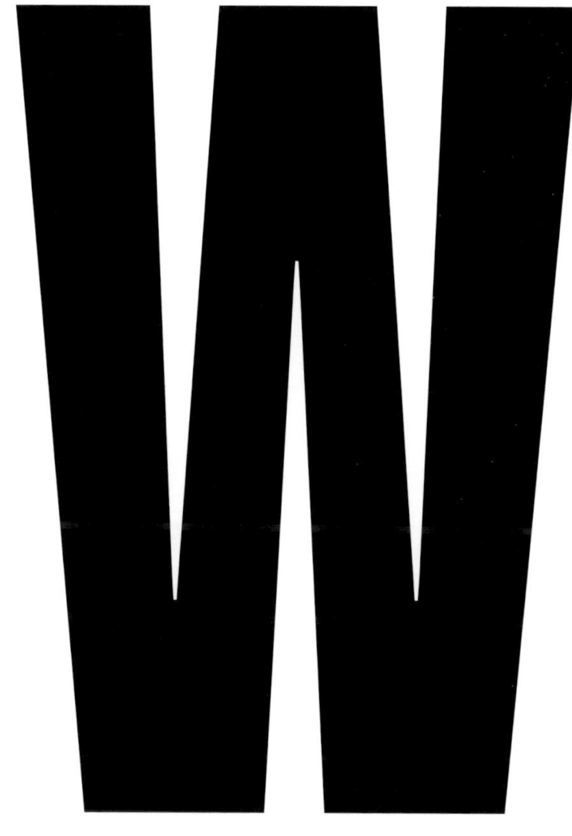

Was it luck or the obvious outcome? How can we possibly explain in any rational way why it is so simple to move from sausage skins to tennis courts? To understand how Babolat turned the sport into its most faithful partner, we have to step back a little in time to the 19th century when the aristocracy's favourite ball game was the *jeu de paume*. For hundreds of years, kings and dukes in France and England had played the game in galleries, first with their bare hands, then wearing leather gloves and eventually using the very first racquets. These racquets were made entirely of wood, had a slightly curved head, and were handmade, as were the cork-filled balls. At that time *jeu de paume* was the sport of gentlemen, and tennis was its direct heir, finally making its first appearance in 1874 thanks to one man, Major Walter Clopton Wingfield. A descendent of the Duke of Wingfield and a former officer in the Indian army, when he retired to his London residence he found he had too much time on his hands. Passionate about sport, which was in his genes, he began playing *jeu de paume* at home. Frustrated by the existing rules, he decided to modernise and codify the game, after which

OPENING In 1874, Major Walter Clopton Wingfield invents a form of tennis played on grass called Sphairistikè, meaning "the art of the ball" in Greek. He is recognised as the inventor of modern tennis.

OPPOSITE PAGE Gentleman playing jeu de paume (nowadays known as real tennis) during Henri III's reign. Drawing, Paris, 1586.

he adapted it to be played on grass with rubber balls. It's fair to say the Major played well but, to be honest, he was not a champion. His record was modest but his creativity knew no bounds. In his garden, he created the first courts with a net, designed racquets and balls, developing his own set of specific rules. To begin with, his new sport was saddled with the somewhat challenging name of *sphairistikē*, a Greek word meaning "the art of the ball" and he applied for a patent under this name on 23rd February 1874. After the patent was granted, things moved quickly. The Major marketed his invention by producing a portable kit with a booklet that explained the rules. In the box, the contents of which were both practical and educational, players found four light wooden racquets, a net with posts, as well as strips to mark out the court. The game was an immediate success. The Major's invention was hailed across England, played on the lawns of British homes and taking the place of croquet, which had previously been popular. Unsurprisingly, though, the name of this new fashionable sport was difficult to remember and its rules remained complex, even incomplete. Major Clopton therefore renamed his invention Lawn Tennis and agreed to standardize the rules with the racquet sports authority. That's how it really took off, with the first ever Wimbledon tournament held only three years later in 1877, but how did Babolat become involved in it all? The French company entered the game in 1875, a year after tennis was born.

THE ORIGINS OF THE WORD "TENNIS"

The word "Tennis" is actually derived from "tenez," the imperative of the French verb "tenir." When playing *jeu de paume*, Anglo-Saxons adopted the habit of calling out "tenez," old French for "take, receive," just before serving the ball. English pronunciation slightly distorted the word, gradually leading to the game becoming known in English as "Tennis."

FROM SAUSAGES TO TENNIS COURTS

As the first exchanges were taking place on English courts, Babolat was operating in a totally different world: that of developing natural gut casings for sausages. The Babolat & Monnier establishments were the leaders in this field and, every day in Lyon, their teams would set out on horseback to collect the small intestine waste of animals from nearby slaughterhouse, which was then reshaped and recycled for a totally different use. The daily routine of Pierre Babolat and his team revolved not only around sausage casings, which was their speciality, but also making strings for musical instruments and surgical threads. In the fields of charcuterie, music and health, the firm enjoyed an unparalleled reputation, and its expertise was held in high regard. Then, one morning in 1875, Pierre Babolat received a rather surprising letter from George Gibson Bussey, a music-loving Englishman who made tennis racquets and who had heard about Babolat from across the Channel. His request was both simple and unprecedented: he wanted the Lyon-based company to manufacture the very first strings for his wooden racquets. He was keen to create a revolutionary string that would be as good as the finest cello strings on the market. Pierre Babolat knew nothing about sport and even less about tennis; nevertheless, he accepted the request immediately despite the physical constraints it involved. Simply imagining such a string was a technological challenge as it had to be long enough to cover the racquet frame, that is to say 21 feet (or over 6 metres) long. It also required a certain resistance to wear and tear, and that parameter was a real leap into the unknown. Unlike a guitar, the strings of a tennis racquet are not plucked or strummed, but struck, with the strings acting as a compact 'trampoline' to return the ball. While this presented a real challenge at the time, Babolat had already set its sights on innovation and Pierre saw this as a fantastic opportunity to diversify and open up new horizons. After weeks of work and numerous tests carried out in his warehouses in Lyon, he pioneered a cutting-edge technique to develop his very first tennis racquet string, just one year after the sport made its official debut. It saw the birth of the first natural gut string and the beginning of the Babolat tennis story. No one could have imagined that this partnership would give birth to the greatest of adventures.

RIGHT The visionary Pierre Babolat set up the family business in Lyon in 1875.

OPPOSITE PAGE Part of the history of tennis is forever linked with this team of *boyaudiers* (tripe butchers). Babolat's stringing operations have evolved in parallel with the size of the factory in Lyon.

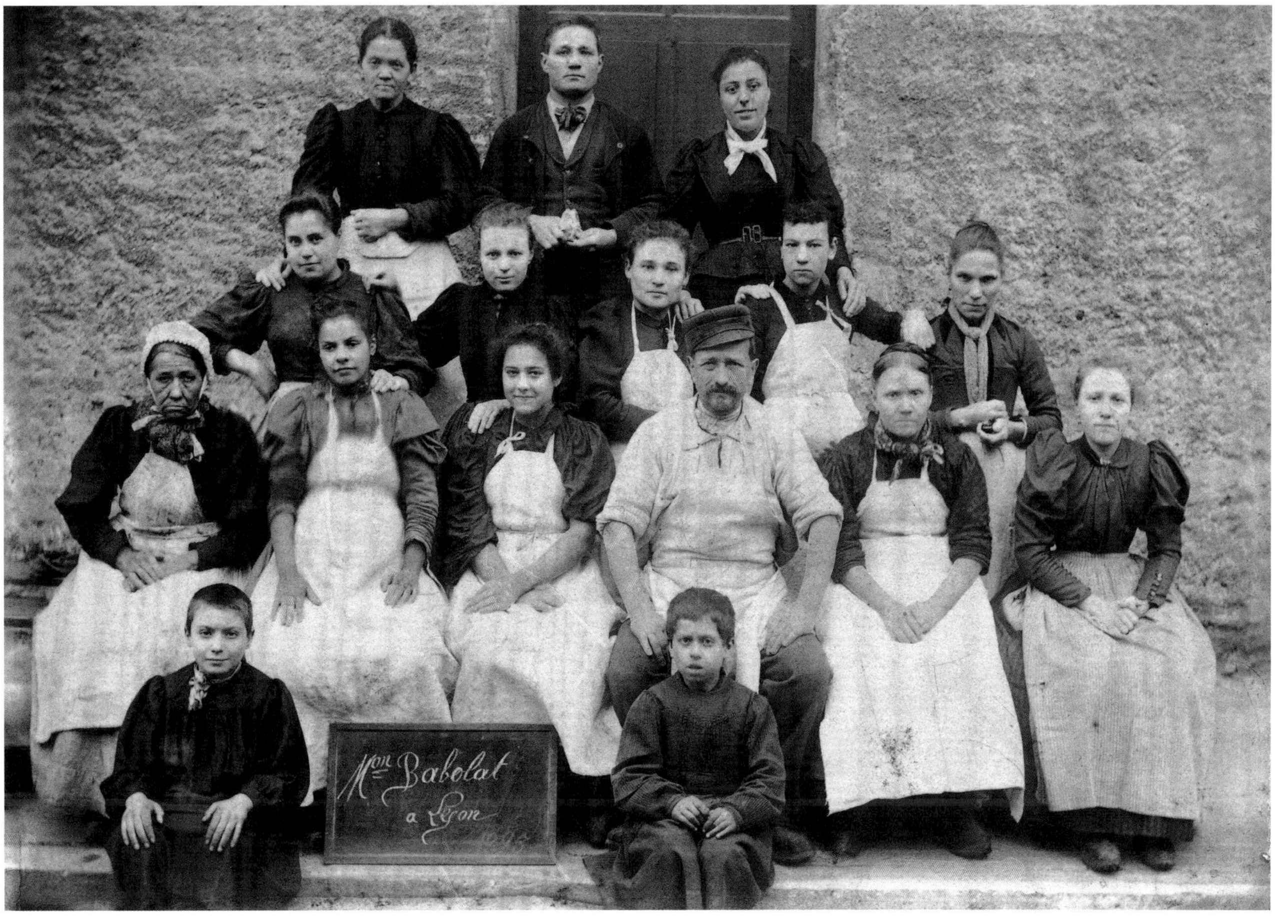
Mon Babolat
a Lyon

BABOLAT-MAILLOT-WITT
Vue d'ensemble des usines de Lyon
1885
1926
1921
1929
jusqu'à 1873

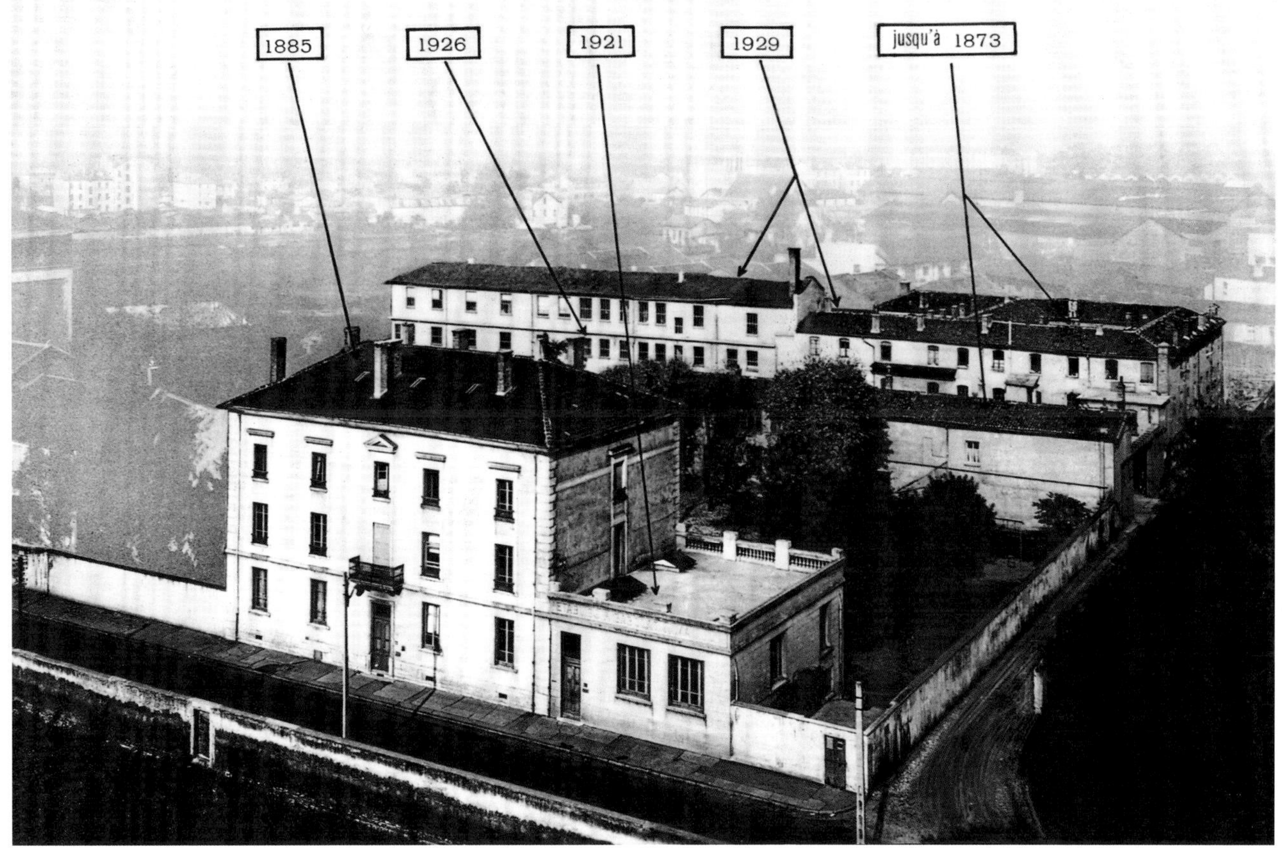

MORE THAN 150 YEARS OF HISTORY

What if Babolat was more than 150 years old? Although the epic tennis story began in 1875, the company's roots date back to early 19th century Lyon, in what today is the city's 1st arrondissement. It was there that an Italian lute maker called Savaresse, the son of an immigrant, established his string workshop. His small shop was next door to a large butcher's shop that was also an abattoir and this was a stroke of luck as he could collect the intestines of sheep, lengths of which he used to make strings. Later, at the height of the Industrial Revolution, Savaresse began a collaboration with Jean-François Monnier, who in 1848 continued the venture on his own, producing strings for musical instruments, sausage casings for butchers and surgical threads. Jean-François Monnier soon joined forces with his son-in-law, Pierre Babolat, whose parents were pork butchers. In 1875 they moved the company to the Gerland district, where, by chance, they were soon joined by the city's abattoirs, located in the Tony-Garnier Hall.

Parisette
Le seul vrai Protecteur
Der einzig richtige Schutz
The sole true protector
El único verdadero protector
Mouiller avant l'usage
Vor gebrauch anfeuchten
Moisten before using
Mojar antes de usarlo
INDUBO. PARIS
DÉPOSÉ
A. Rivolier-paris

ORDONNANCE DU ROI
Autorisant le transfert, dans la Maison du Sr. Pitat, sise quai de Javelle à Grenelle, de la
FABRIQUE
de Cordes à Instruments
du Sr. François Savaresse.

Louis-Philippe, Roi des Français, à tous présents et à venir, Salut.

Fait au Palais de Neuilly, le 23 Mai 1843.
Signé: Louis Philippe.

ABOVE Advertising for Parisette, a condom made from natural casings.

RIGHT King Louis Philippe's ordinance of 23 May 1843 authorizing the relocation of the SAVARESSE company, which manufactures hand-ground casing strings and bare strings, and begins production of spun strings.

NATURAL CASINGS OF THE BEST QUALITY

In 1875, casings were used for a wide variety of purposes, not just as skins for sausages, chipolotas and merguez, but also for making stringed and keyboard musical instruments. They were used in more unusual ways too, such as to produce a dried film to seal perfume bottles and even for manufacturing condoms. At the time, casings were a highly prized raw material, considered the royal seal of approval, no less, of traditional charcuterie. The natural sheep's gut originally chosen to make the first tennis racquet strings was, therefore, a product with a fine noble heritage. The animal's small intestine is not just of exceptional quality and texture, but the must-have, in other words the very best. Unlike linen and cotton strings, natural gut also adds a "motor" and "trampoline" effect as it stores energy and releases it into the ball. Babolat realised quickly that the strings were a fundamental part of a racquet, you could describe them as its lungs. Indeed, they are the only part that comes into contact with the ball and that only for the briefest moment, estimated at between 3 and 7 thousandths of a second, but this time is crucial as all the criteria must be met. The strings are the equivalent of the racquet's engine and are responsible for 50% of its performance. The transition from gut to string is of necessity a meticulous process, almost an exercise in design, requiring patience, skill, method and, above all, a lot of animal matter. To give an example, at the time it took six sheep to produce a single string and, although the celebrated sheep guts were chosen initially, they were not ideally suited to the specific nature of tennis, due to their low tensile strength and short length. Gradually they were replaced by cow intestines, which have a serous membrane containing collagen and elastic fibres and are better in terms of comfort and performance when playing. Babolat quickly learned from his early experiments.

ABOVE In 1925, the diameter of the strings was obtained using polishing benches.

FOLLOWING PAGES The quality of Babolat's VS strings is determined in these workshops. Each end of the sheep gut is checked before being cut and each string is spun by hand.

BABOLAT

AND THE FIRST CHAMPIONS

1920

1960

DURING THE 1920S, TENNIS BECAME THE FASHIONABLE SPORT AND BABOLAT'S RACQUET STRINGS WERE A MUST-HAVE, IN THE SAME WAY AS THE LATEST OUTFIT OR NECKLACE. THE NATURAL GUT STRINGS, PIONEERED BY THE FRENCH BRAND, WERE IN DEMAND EVERYWHERE BECAUSE THEIR UNIQUE COMBINATION OF QUALITY, STRENGTH AND RELIABILITY APPEALED TO BOTH CLUB PLAYERS AND THOSE WHO WON MAJOR CHAMPIONSHIPS. THE STRINGS COULD BE FOUND IN EVERY SPORTS BAG AND AT VICTORIES BOTH GREAT AND SMALL. IN FRANCE, THE REVOLUTIONARY STRINGS BECAME PART OF THE GREATEST OF ALL TRIUMPHS, THOSE OF THE 'MUSKETEERS', A QUARTET OF FOUR EXCEPTIONAL PLAYERS WHO MADE FRANCE'S DREAMS COME TRUE BETWEEN THE TWO WORLD WARS: RENÉ LACOSTE, HENRI COCHET, JEAN BOROTRA AND JACQUES BRUGNON.

OPENING René Lacoste at a Davis Cup match in 1928.

OPPOSITE PAGE Poster for Babolat-Maillot racquet strings, 1948.

In cafés and restaurants, they were the talk of the town; on court, dressed in jackets and long trousers, they triumphed. Their precious racquets, strung with Babolat strings, gave them formidable ammunition and the inter-war years was the ideal backdrop for the exploits of these Musketeers, four masters of their game and a perfect embodiment of the conquering spirit driving France at that time. It seemed that nothing was impossible for this band of gentlemen who were filled with patriotic fervour, especially when facing the Americans who until then had been considered invincible. On 10 September 1927, the Musketeers won the Davis cup, the most prestigious team competition in the world, beating the Americans. It was a resounding and unexpected feat but, above all, it was a victory that propelled them to iconic status. Their legend was born and their glory everlasting with René Lacoste, Henri Cochet, Jean Borotra and Jacques Brugnon going on to win 54 Grand Slam titles between the four of them, and as many ovations. In a world where tennis was still reserved for a certain élite—those who applauded while wearing gloves and threw their hats in the air as they cheered—

ABOVE The Musketeers (from left to right, Jacques Brugnon, Henri Cochet, René Lacoste and Jean Borotra) pose with their racquets and their Babolat strings at Le Pré Catelan restaurant.

OPPOSITE PAGE 1930s tourist poster designed by Roger Broders for the Monte-Carlo tennis tournament in Monaco.

ROGER BRODERS

MONTE·CARLO

the Musketeers, together with another legendary champion called Suzanne Lenglen, made the sport more popular. They began by modernizing it, actively getting involved in developing the sport's equipment, whereby the racquet became an extension of the human arm, a sword that enabled them to win their matches. The racquet's strings became a key element in this arsenal during play and, here, Babolat clearly won the match. The company becme the preferred brand of star players because the comfort, the strengh, and durability of natural gut strings have never been equalled. Driven by their common desire for success, champions worked hand in hand with the expertise of Babolat's technicians to powerful effect. The family business developed even more sophisticated natural gut strings when, in 1925, Pierre Babolat's forty-year-old invention underwent its most groundbreaking evolution with the birth of the VS quality natural gut string.

THE GENESIS OF THE VS STRING

When tennis experienced its first rush of popularity after the 1914–1918 war, everyone went crazy for Babolat strings. Natural gut was like a polished jewel, a cherished accessory for stringing the world's wooden racquets and equally sought after by modest players as well as advanced. However, when the sport became more mainstream and the rules were modernized, there was a major boom in the demand for equipment. As players learned more and more about their sport, they also became more demanding over what they wanted and these demands led to technical refinements. It is champions who are often the driving force behind such developments and when they wanted thinner strings with higher tension they turned to Albert Babolat, who had taken over the family business in the early 1920s. He was just as much a visionary as his elder brother and he set about finding a sustainable alternative to meet these new demands. Surrounding himself with experts, he built his team and, thanks to extensive feedback, created a string that would change the history of tennis: a VS quality string made from natural gut with unique features. Simultaneously the company became Babolat-Maillot-Witt and would be an enduring template in the tennis world. The charcuterie days seemed long gone.

VS — A CODE NAME

The principle behind the design of this most advanced string was simple. The Musketeers were given a selection of samples to try in alphabetical order and over time the gang of four—René, Henri, Jean and Jacques—made their choice. After a lot of to-ing and fro-ing, sample V came out top as the best quality and, at that time, VS stood for *Very Superior* in English. The landmark reference VS was, in fact, nothing more than a code name and was decided against as a trade name. The reason the Musketeers liked this one so much was it offered unprecedented elasticity, striking power and resistance. Its sturdiness and ability to withstand the test of time have made the VS string a model of its kind, winning over customers worldwide. Without realising it, these samples with their rather primitive technical name kickstarted one of the most dazzling pages in the history of tennis. Ever since, Babolat strings have been made in France, at a factory in Ploërmel, Brittany.

ABOVE Albert Babolat continues the family's work by creating the VS string which becomes a global benchmark.

OPPOSITE PAGE As with a piece of statement jewellery, the VS becomes the accessory that every player at the time was desperate to have. Its strength and durability made the string a world beater.

FOLLOWING PAGES In 1927, France beats the USA in the final of the Davis Cup using the VS string.

VS
made in
france

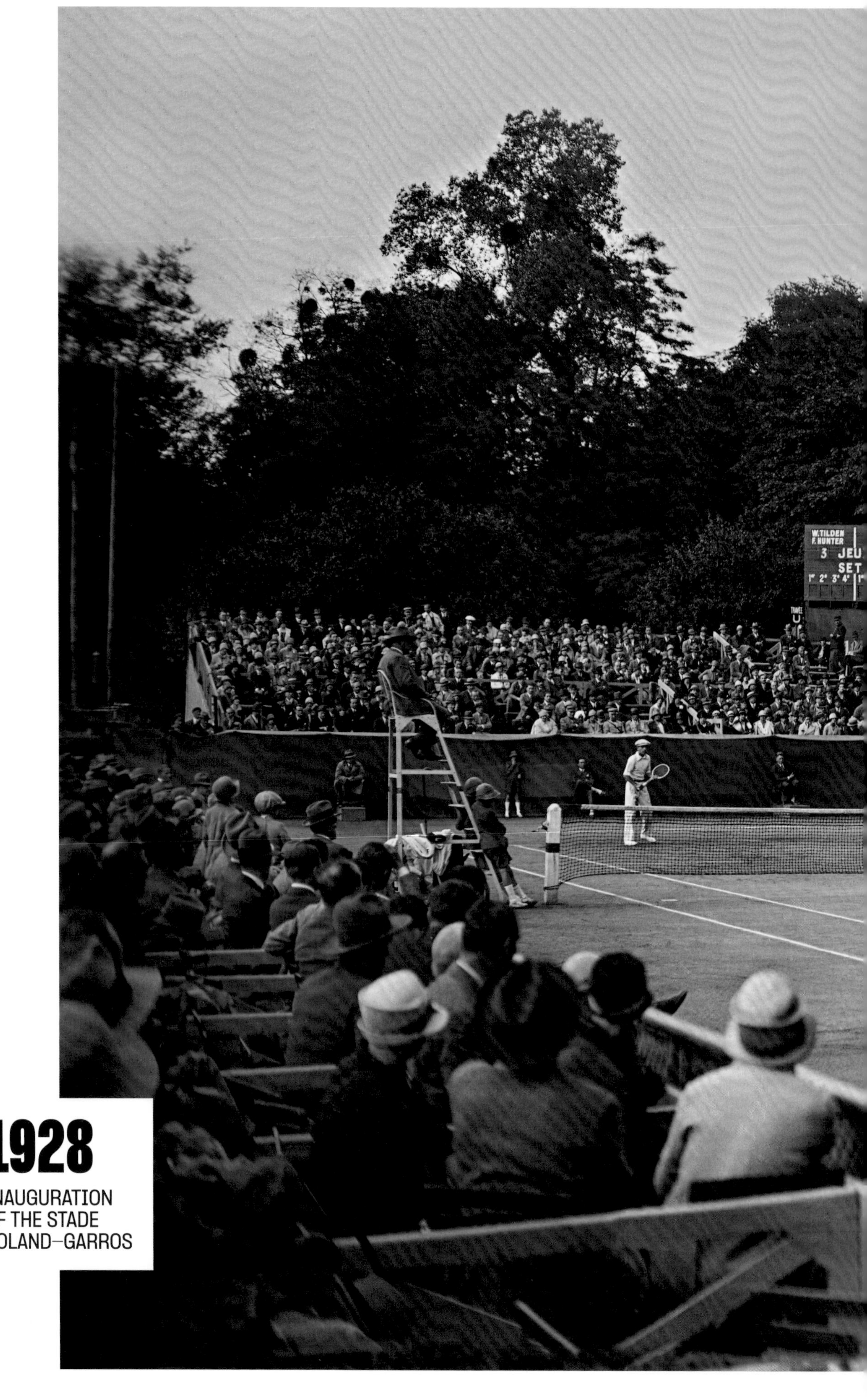

1928

INAUGURATION
OF THE STADE
ROLAND-GARROS

ICONS OF AN ERA

THE MUSKETEERS, ALL OF THEM FANS OF BABOLAT

RENÉ LACOSTE

Nicknamed "the crocodile" not just for the crocodile skin Louis Vuitton suitcase he carried everywhere he went, but also for his style of play, which was sometimes described as minimalist as he simply returned the ball tenaciously without making a mistake. An influential man in his time, he also developed several major inventions: the tennis ball firing machine, the anti-vibration shock absorber and the steel racquet. He later launched his own clothing range, using a small crocodile emblem as his logo. With his unflagging pursuit of progress, he made a major contribution to the development of Babolat products, in particular the creation of the VS. He won seven major singles tournaments, including Roland-Garros, a title he earned three times.

JEAN BOROTRA

He was nicknamed "the bounding Basque," in reference to his somewhat unconventional style on court. He was an attacking player in perpetual motion, whose acrobatics delighted crowds and threw opponents off balance. With the help of the VS string and his frenetic ingenuity, this man, who had discovered tennis by chance during a trip to England to study the language, went on to claim 18 Grand Slam titles.

JACQUES BRUGNON

Known as "Toto," he was the oldest of the four. He impressed with his ability to remain calm and in control. He was, mostly notably, a great doubles player, winning six titles at Roland–Garros and five in Australia, where he distinguished himself alongside Suzanne Lenglen in the mixed doubles. He was also an innovator, inventing the lifted lob, a shot that has become a formidable weapon in modern tennis.

HENRI COCHET

He was known as "the magician" since it was said he could achieve the impossible on court. The most successful of the Musketeers, he was also the only one not to have grown up in a middle–class environment, which was unusual at the time. The son of a secretary of the FCL tennis club in Lyon–Caluire, he triumphed in seven Grand Slam events, armed with his "magic wand" equipped with its VS strings.

SUZANNE LENGLEN

Known as *"la divine"* in France, she was the first great star of women's tennis and her game, her looks and her level of play made her a celebrity in her day. She first became an icon in England before conquering France. She knocked out her opponents with powerful shots, dazzling them with her smash, serve and volley. But it was also her elegance, combined with a touch of daring, that marked her era. In the city, she wore haute couture dresses. On court, she twirled around in short, pleated tennis skirts that finished just above her knees. Suzanne Lenglen was a woman ahead of her time, who was comfortable wearing soft materials and sleeveless tops, which gave her the freedom to jump and volley as she pleased. She also stood out by sporting an orange tulle headband at a time when white was de rigueur. Her sole nod to convention was when it came to choosing strings for her racquet—ones marked "VS Babolat," of course!

ABOVE In 1927, Jean Borotra, nicknamed "the bounding Basque", raises France's profile with his Babolat strings during his match against Romania.

OPPOSITE PAGE Jacques Brugnon at the 1939 Wimbledon tournament, where he and Jean Borotra clinch third place in the men's doubles.

PAGE 37 In 1927, France's victory in the Davis Cup against the USA marks the pinnacle of the golden generation of French tennis, represented by the "Musketeers". The Babolat & Maillot brands are linked with this prestigious success.

DON'T FORGET THAT THE "VS" PLAYED ITS PART IN THE MUSKETEERS' VICTORY IN THE DAVIS CUP IN 1927. IN MEMORY OF THIS GREAT ERA.

— Henri Cochet

Durant ma carrière de joueur amateur, j'ai eu l'occasion d'essayer plus de 15 marques de cordes pour mes raquettes, aucune ne m'a donné autant de satisfaction au point de vue rendement et au point de vue régularité de fabrication que les cordes BABOLAT & MAILLOT.

Elles m'ont toujours conduit à tous les succès et c'est avec elles que j'ai joué tous mes matches de Coupe Davis.

Il va de soi que, comme joueur professionnel, je fais confiance aux cordes BABOLAT & MAILLOT *qui équipent toutes mes raquettes.*

Cochet

"Henri Cochet — Novembre 1933".

1926

SUZANNE LENGLEN WINS THE MATCH OF THE CENTURY AGAINST HELEN WILLS MOODY

PREVIOUS PAGES René Lacoste during the Davis Cup meeting between France and Romania in 1927.

ABOVE Suzanne Lenglen, nicknamed the Divine, was an icon of her age. She loved loose clothing, short sleeves and skirts that allowed her to move more freely, something that was revolutionary at the time.

OPPOSITE PAGE During a tour of the USA and Canada, Suzanne Lenglen played Mary K. Browne 38 times from 1926 to 1927 and won every one of the matches.

SUZANNE LENGLEN

Nicknamed the "Divine", she challenged both the rules of tennis and those of fashion. Almost 100 years before Rafael Nadal, she was already wearing a handband.

RAFAEL NADAL

With his tanktop, long shorts, headband and looking like a warrior ready for battle, he revolutionised the genre. Rafa's unique style of play has left its mark on the story of tennis.

BOL
PROTÈGE
VOS

THE ADVANTAGES OF VS

But why is VS so good? The reason is obvious—it's because natural gut allows you to play better! The strings' feel for the ball is incomparable, offering that rare and dreamed of sensation that the ball seemingly sticks to the racquet for longer. This flexibility at the point of impact gives every player greater control but VS's other major advantage is the ability of the strings to remain as taut as on day one. This unique quality of elasticity is made possible by collagen from the intestines of cows, which resist the contractions and stretches of the intestine. It is this collagen that provides the special sensations produced by the strings, both of power and making the arm feel comfortable. It is no coincidence, therefore, that VS is recommended for players who suffer from arm pain, such as the notorious tennis elbow.

In the past, strings made from natural gut were the only option for racquets but, today, as the game has evolved, its qualities are mostly used at the highest level by combining it with a polyester. In this instance, we are talking about a hybrid string that combines comfort and durability. As the gut string is a natural product, it is important to weave it in a way that respects its nature, avoiding excessive friction up and down, without bending it and using a professional stringing machine. It is the particular skill of specialists who offer this premium stringing to their clients.

For decades, Babolat has understood how to refine its flagship product to ensure it continues to appeal to all masters of the racquet, whether champions or amateurs. Modernised and now sturdier thanks to a specific process, the natural gut string retains its age-old qualities, while offering higher performance. As a result, VS is the string of choice for the world's greatest champions—winners of over 150 Grand Slams in total between them! —and club players alike.

MAKING STRINGS FROM CAT GUT IS JUST A MYTH

When they developed the first strings, Pierre Babolat and his teams favoured using sheep's gut but, during the late 1970s, everything changed. As racquets got larger and the tension of the strings tighter, it was cow gut that was finally preferred. A cow's small intestine is 50 metres long and is longer and stronger than a sheep's, which measures just 30 metres. Pig's gut was never even considered as it cannot provide the necessary resistance and, as for cats, using the infamous catgut is simply part of the legend and for one obvious reason—size. A cat's intestine measures just 1.3 metres, while a single racquet string requires 12 metres. Just imagine how many cats would be needed to string one racquet!

OPPOSITE PAGE At the 1952 Salon des Sports, a giant bottle of Babol varnish was on display as a reminder of the importance of protecting strings to prolong their life.

LEFT During tournaments, Babolat staff work on players' racquets to meet their individual needs and adapt their equipment accordingly.

ABOVE Natural strings treated with the protection All Season.

PAGE 46 Advertising calendar from the 1950s (left) and "Mousquetaires" natural string (right).

PAGE 47 Advertising poster from the 1950s.

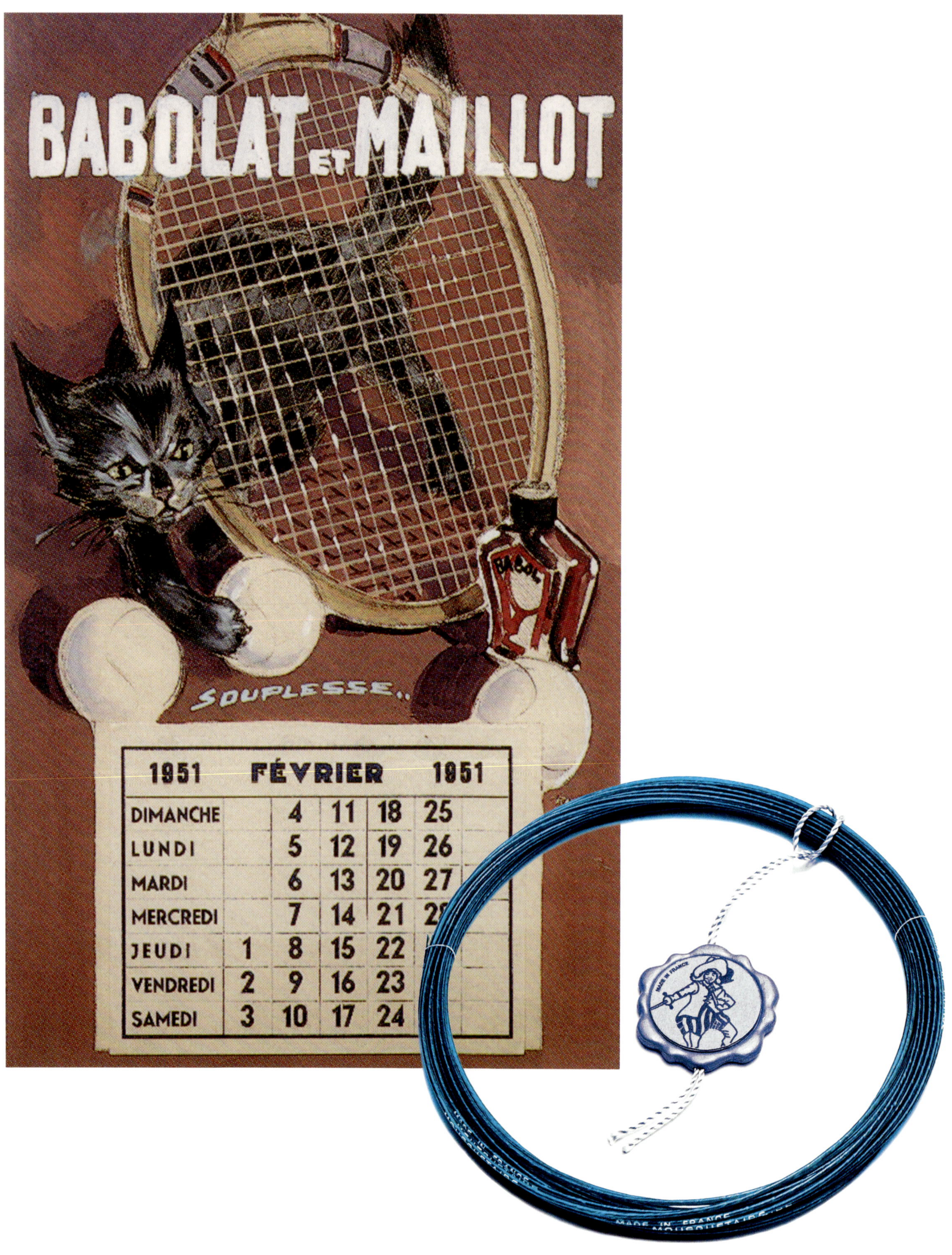
BABOLAT ET MAILLOT
BABOL
SOUPLESSE..
1951 FÉVRIER 1951
DIMANCHE 4 11 18 25
LUNDI 5 12 19 26
MARDI 6 13 20 27
MERCREDI 7 14 21
JEUDI 1 8 15 22
VENDREDI 2 9 16 23
SAMEDI 3 10 17 24
MADE IN FRANCE

BABOL
BABOLAT
ET
MAILLOT

PLOËRMEL
WHERE THE NATURAL GUT STRINGS ARE MADE

One hundred and fifty years after its invention, the natural gut string still exists and Babolat has never stopped improving it. This flagship product is made in France, in the heart of Brittany at the Ploërmel factory in the Morbihan region. Since 1979, teams have been keeping alive the traditional skill that has shaped the development of tennis since its beginnings. Here, we reveal the secrets behind the manufacture of the world's most famous string: the Babolat VS.

TOP The method used to make natural gut strings has remained unchanged for 150 years. This artisanal craftsmanship is the pride of Babolat.

BOTTOM Sanding strings by hand during the drying stage.

OPPOSITE PAGE Two operators clean off excess grease by hand and scrape away any remaining flaws.

To find this vital place, you have to leave Rennes and drive south-west for an hour. On arrival, you will find a large, white warehouse in a rather anonymous industrial area, but it is from here that some of the greatest triumphs have emerged. Neither Borg, Noah, Sampras, Mauresmo or Bartoli has ever set foot here but they owe some of their success to this place. And what do you need to get in? Just a hair-net and protective clothing. The first impression you get in the operations centre is not something you see but a distinctive odour. The curious smell that bombards your senses is of bovine gut being processed. It is the same type of smell as when paper pulp is being made. Once the initial effect subsides, you can concentrate on what matters. Here, you will meet men and women working with their hands on the small intestines of cows. There is a frenzy and a kind of passion about the people who have carried on the traditional trade of the "boyaudier" (tripe dresser) since the origins of the company and the establishment of the VS Babolat brand. To develop this exceptional product, it was necessary to have a detailed approach but, first of all, quality raw material was needed. Brittany was the obvious choice for this due to its abundant greenery, rainy climate and....exceptional cows. It is true that the Brittany cattle are healthier and their gut of better quality than elsewhere in France. In the area around Ploëmel, a total of seven abattoirs have entered into partnership with Babolat, in Brittany, Sarthe or the Pays de la Loire. A total of two cows and fifteen people are needed to produce a single string and no time is wasted as a steady rhythm is maintained.

While the company has always adapted to the changing face of tennis, its basic approach has not changed. The secret of its success is still the same, a skilful combination of painstaking work and downtime. It takes four weeks to make the finest strings and produce the best finish from beginning to end. There are numerous stages with the gut passing from hand to hand as it undergoes the necessary transformations.

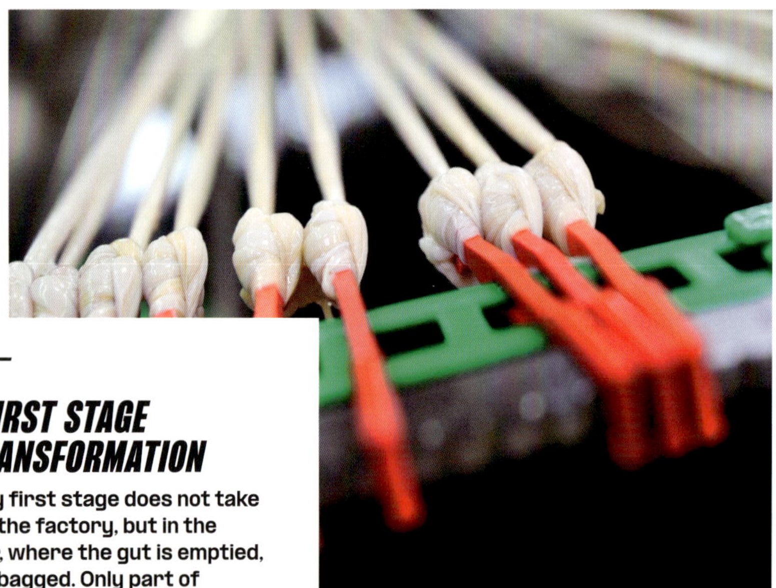

1—
THE FIRST STAGE OF TRANSFORMATION

The very first stage does not take place in the factory, but in the abattoir, where the gut is emptied, cut and bagged. Only part of the intestine is retained, a strip measuring 4 cm wide and around 50 metres long, which is then delivered to Ploëmel where it is stored in large refrigerators.

2—
MEASURING – SKINNING – QUALITY INSPECTION

On a large table, sixteen strips are cut, each measuring 12.65 m. The reason for this is to allow a little extra for the finished string, which will be exactly 12 metres long. With a quick and confident movement, that day's operator will then divide the gut in two, retaining only the outer, most resistant coating. The other part is set aside. The strips then pass under a UV index of 3 where they are inspected for any kind of possible defect, whether grease, cuts or imperfections.

3—
TYING WORKSTATIONS

Here the strips are divided into groups of six or seven, then tied at the 12 metre mark. It is only when this stage is reached that we can start talking about strings. The main challenge lies in not tangling these ribbons, which are all tied with a hook. It takes an entire day to reach this stage and each string remains separate.

4—
CHEMICAL TREATMENT

Over the course of 24 hours, the strings are then cleaned, treated and immersed in nine successive baths, the purpose of which is to remove grease from each string and whiten it to remove the orange colour from the strips.

5—
DRYING

In another very large room, there is a wide drying rack. It is here that one thousand six hundred strings, which have been removed from the treatment baths, are moved to undergo one of the most important stages in string production: drying. Each string is mechanically twisted for around ten minutes—giving it the equivalent of more than a thousand turns—before everything is left to dry for 24 hours in a humid atmosphere at 25°C and initially with 80% relative humidity, to ensure the drying process is a gentle one. Meanwhile, two operators clean off excess grease and scrape away any remaining flaws by hand, a process that takes them an hour to inspect four hundred strings. The strings are then sheathed and stored flat like long spaghetti, for three weeks. This valuable time allows the strings to dry thoroughly and stabilise. Nothing is left to chance with each batch being traceable to the slaughterhouse and the week of collection.

6—
FINISHING

The large packages are then transferred to a second part of the factory that since 2008 has been located in Brittany. Prior to that, the final stages were carried out at Babolat's historic Gerland site in Lyon. Completion takes place on automated production lines. Depending on the diameter selected, each string is measured individually by laser and, if necessary, the surface of the string is sanded by grinding machines to achieve the corresponding diameter that is measured in hundredths of a millimetre. The string is then cleaned, coloured as required and dried again using a customised machining system. It then passes through a varnishing bath to strengthen its resistance to the gut's "enemy"—humidity. There is one final quality control check where someone scrutinises the string for defects such as grease spirals, beading, black spots or pieces of straw. If the string does not pass, it is downgraded to second best and will not bear the VS stamp. Multiple tests are then carried out using a mechanical workbench or with a stringing machine to check for resistance or varnish problems.

7—
CONDITIONING

The strings are rolled by hand before being packed, which is one more opportunity to spot any final defects either by eye or touch. Every effort is made to avoid the "orange peel" effect that occurs when a string is not completely smooth. The finished article is then packed in bags identical to those used for foods to be freeze-dried or needing protection from UV light, before being shipped worldwide.

ABOVE To avoid the strings tangling, they are attached to a hook at the tying station.

OPPOSITE PAGE The strings are rolled before being conditioned then shipped to all parts of the world.

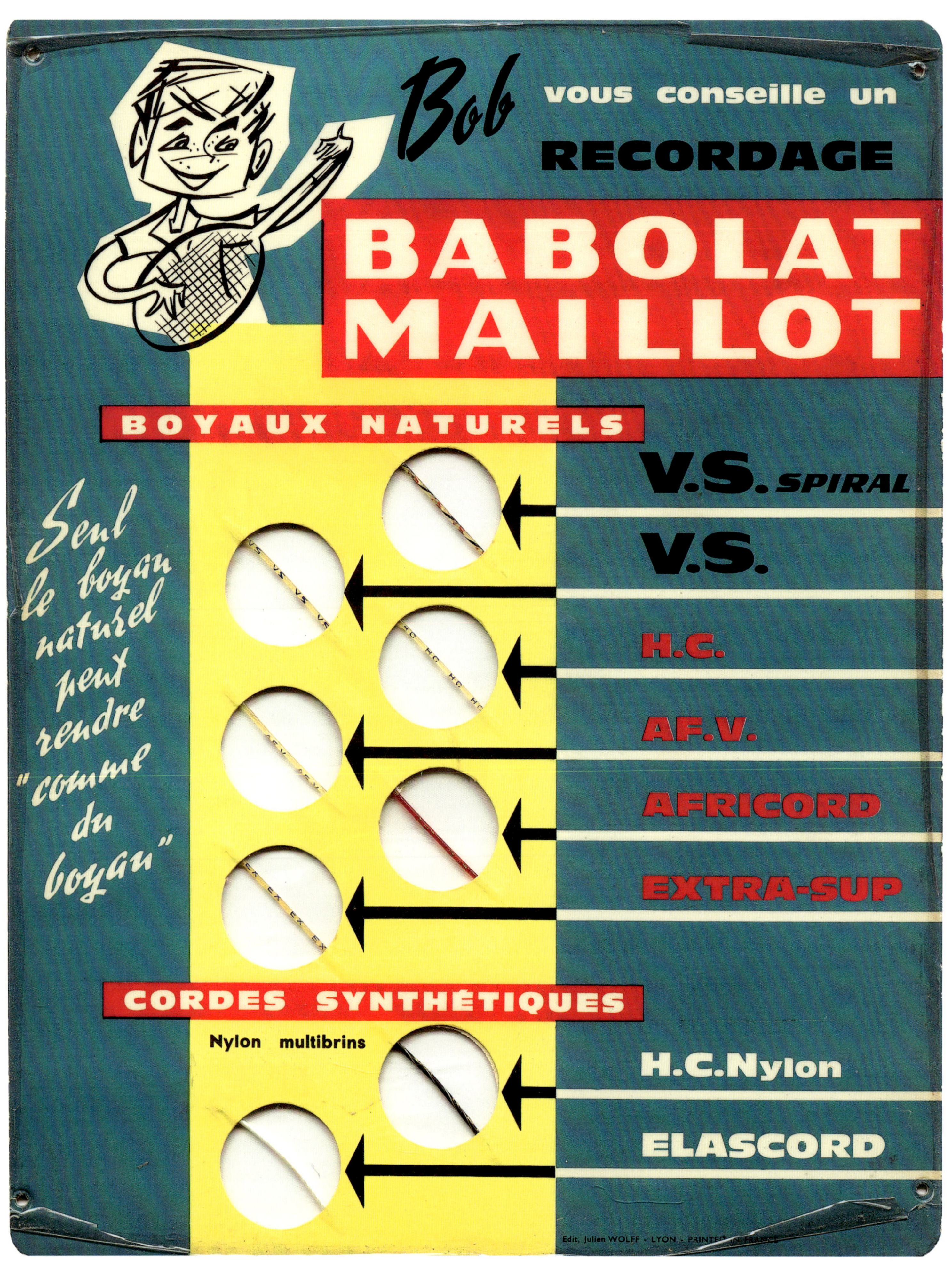
Bob vous conseille un
RECORDAGE
BABOLAT
MAILLOT
BOYAUX NATURELS
Seul le boyau naturel peut rendre "comme du boyau"
V.S. SPIRAL
V.S.
H.C.
AF.V.
AFRICORD
EXTRA-SUP
CORDES SYNTHÉTIQUES
Nylon multibrins
H.C.Nylon
ELASCORD

THE SYNTHETIC REVOLUTION — 1955 : THE INVENTION OF ELASCORD

During the 1950s tennis continued its remarkable growth in popularity. Shortly after the traumas of World War II, people began focusing on well-being and leisure activities. Playing sports became the best way to enjoy themselves and they played tennis in their free time and on holiday, with family or friends, and it was not just the elite. Members of the middle classes took up this exhilarating activity, clubs began to multiply, which heralded the arrival of sport for the masses and an endorphin boom.

As interest grew, the pace of matches intensified and the game gathered pace with shots becoming faster and more accurate. Players whose muscles were changing demanded something new. After Pierre and Albert, it was Paul who had taken the helm at Babolat. As a front row witness to this evolution, he continued innovating by devising ever more advanced equipment that was, most importantly, accessible to all. Babolat came up with the inspired idea of creating Elascord, his first synthetic nylon string made of polyamide and polyurethane, which had the added advantage of being cheaper to produce. For, in spite of its success, natural VS gut remained a luxury, being 30 to 50% more expensive than synthetic. However, by launching this revolution, Babolat was able to appeal to even those on the most modest budget by offering an alternative to VS, the maintenance of which could sometimes be a problem. While natural gut is effective on court, it is also very fragile as it is more sensitive to moisture and heat and can break at any time if not properly looked after. Elascord, on the other hand, was designed for amateurs and those who only played tennis occasionally. Thus, Babolat succeeded on all fronts since the brand retained the jewel in its crown, both in the professional world and among champion players, the vast majority of whom continue to use VS.

But Paul Babolat didn't stop there. With tennis now an international phenomenon, he created the world's first company-owned marketing network, rather than simply responding to incoming international demand. It heralded the era of trade and marketing and the brand became familiar to players around the world, from Argentina, Germany, Italy, and the United States to Scandinavia, Eastern Europe, Australia and Japan. The Lyon-based company also began developing comprehensive lines of accessories for racquet frames, including the first grips that absorbed perspiration, in addition to the traditional leather bands.

BABOLISER

At that time, natural gut was unable to withstand moisture and this proved a major problem for players, especially those who lived in humid climates where the damp air penetrated their racquet strings and damaged them. While gut these days is covered with a protective layer of polyurethane that shields it more efficiently from humidity, back then it was necessary to apply a coat of varnish to the strings to preserve them and increase their lifespan. Babol, created by Lyon pharmacist Gyfer, the inventor of mercurochrome (an antiseptic solution) became indispensable and using it an integral part of a player's routine, so much so that the verb "to babolise" entered tennis vocabulary.

OPPOSITE PAGE Advertising panel for Babolat-Maillot racquet strings.

ABOVE Paul Babolat continues the company's tradition of innovation by creating Elascord in 1955.

FOLLOWING PAGES With leather grips or synthetic ones for the handle, Babol and Elastocross, gradually Babolat develops a complete range of accessories.

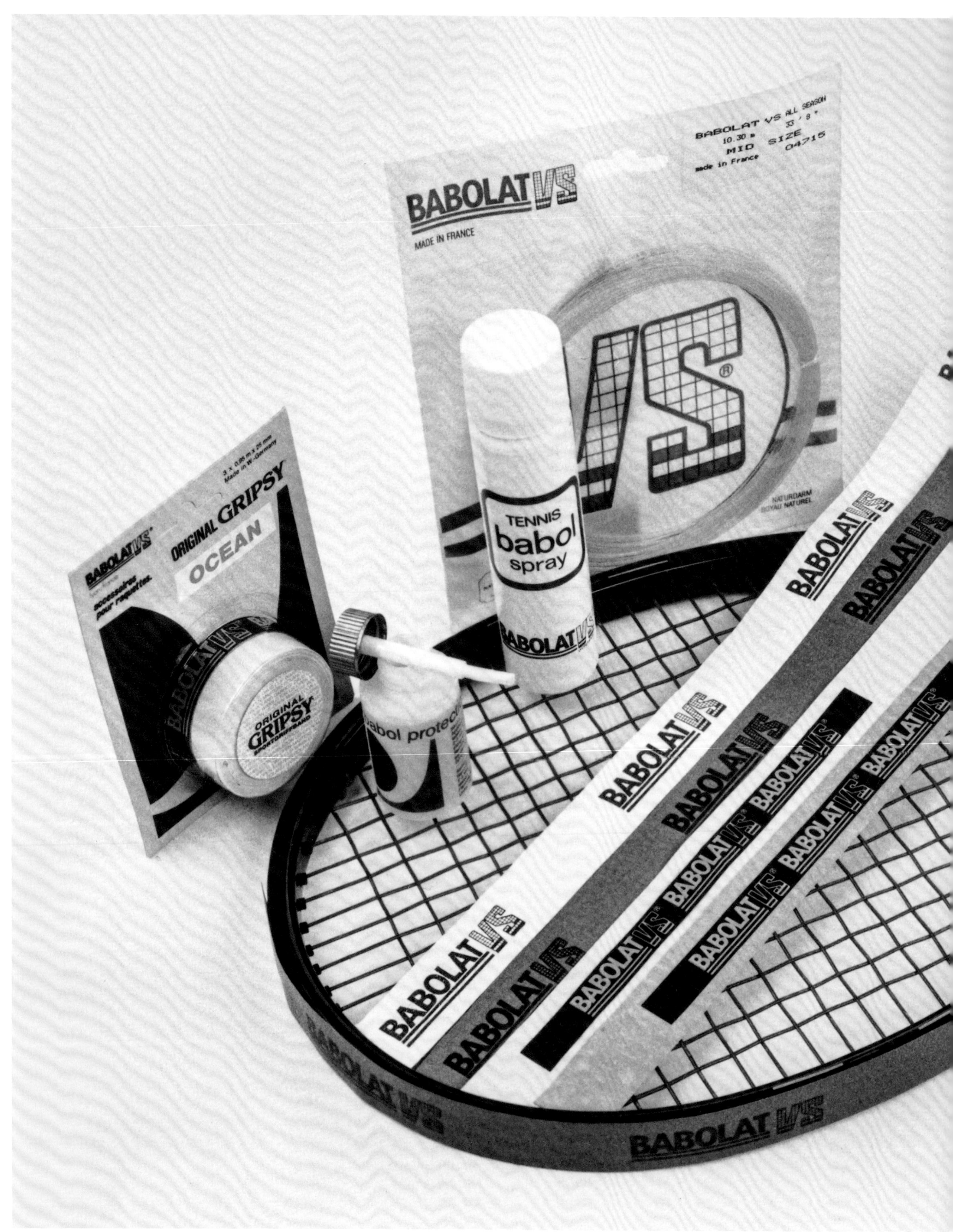
BABOLAT VS ALL SEASON
10.30 m 33'9"
MID SIZE
made in France 04715
BABOLAT VS
MADE IN FRANCE
VS
NATURDARM
BOYAU NATUREL
TENNIS
babol
spray
BABOLAT VS
ORIGINAL GRIPSY
OCEAN
accessoires pour raquettes.
ORIGINAL GRIPSY
babol protect
BABOLAT VS

BABOLAT
HEAD
BABOLAT
PRESTIGE
BABOLAT
BABOLAT

BORG AND NOAH

VS IS SEEN EVERYWHERE

1970

1980

VS
cordes
ennis
BABOLAT
MAILLOT
WITT
VS
boyaux
naturel

A NEW ERA DAWNED FOR BABOLAT WHEN THE ENTIRE WORLD BECAME CAPTIVATED BY AN EXCEPTIONAL CHAMPION. WITH HIS LONG HAIR, CELEBRATED HEADBAND, ANGELIC FEATURES AND HIS UNIQUE STYLE, BJÖRN BORG SWEPT ASIDE ALL THE CONVENTIONS AND REVOLUTIONISED HIS SPORT. IN THE EARLY 1980S, THE SWEDE HAD WON ALL THE MOST PRESTIGIOUS TROPHIES USING VS STRINGS WHICH, FOR HIM, WERE NON-NEGOTIABLE. MANY CHAMPIONS FELT THE SAME, SWEARING BY THE NATURAL GUT, WITH THE RESULT THAT VS BECAME THE MUST-HAVE STRING ON EVERY COURT AROUND THE WORLD.

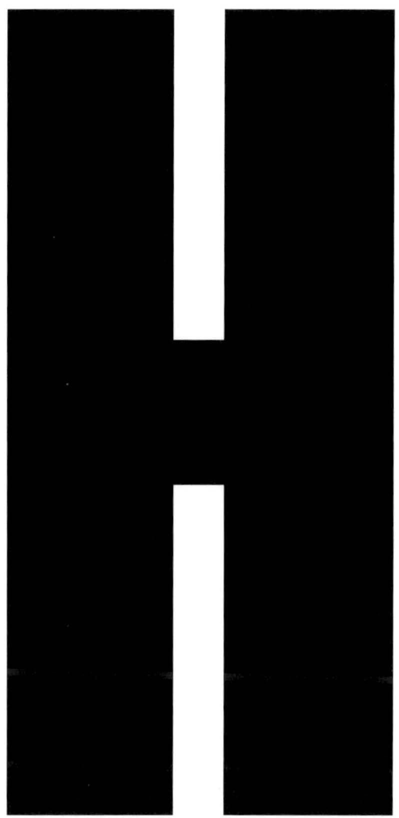

His lightning-fast acceleration, forehand with topspin, double-handed backhand and dazzling passing shots electrified tennis lovers. But at that time, Björn Borg was known primarily for his elusive behaviour and complex personality. It gave the Swede everything he needed to create an aura of mystery and fascination around his name. He was a phenomenon in the game and the rankings. Between 1974 and 1981, Borg won a string of the most prestigious trophies, including a total of six at Roland-Garros—a record that people believed impossible at the time—and five consecutive Wimbledon titles. When he triumphed for the first time on the English grass courts, the reverberations of what he had achieved were so powerful that the barely 17-years-old Björn Borg was immediately propelled to rockstar status. Nicknamed the "ice man" (or "ice-Borg") because of his cool and collected manner on court, he became one of the most popular sportsmen in the world. With him, and his almost mystical inspirations, tennis entered a new dimension. It was a new world where Borg had changed everything, from relations with the media to sponsorship and physical preparation. He also changed the face of tennis from racquets and strings to shoes and balls, with every detail becoming crucial. "All my life, I have played with Babolat's natural gut strings in my racquets as they are the finest quality in terms of equipment,"

OPENING AND OPPOSITE PAGE Björn Borg at Roland-Garros in 1975.

said the champion on every court surface. At that time, Björn Borg had a secret weapon—and the most expensive tool—in his arsenal that he would not have relinquished for anything in the world: his 420-gram wooden-framed racquet made by the Donnay brand and strung with VS natural gut. As a first for him, "VS" appeared in giant capital letters on the strings of the Swedish player's racquet, something that had never happened on a tennis court before.

A DREAM DISPLAY CABINET

Babolat was undeniably associated with the brilliant achievements of Borg's career and his epic success story. Thanks to the advertisement on his racquet's strings, VS became known everywhere and by everyone. As a thank you, and in recognition of his outstanding performances on court, Paul Babolat presented Björn with a "golden VS," an additional trophy for his display cabinet. VS and Borg is a love story, the coming together of passion and routines. For Björn Borg was tenacious by nature, he was superstitious and, as with all champions, he did things his way. Borg kept the tension of his racquets at over 30 kg, which meant the strings often broke, even if he was not playing, and it was not unusual for strings to snap in the middle of the night in his hotel room. However, he could never have dispensed with such a weapon to win and never abandoned those precious, valuable strings. By using natural gut strings to achieve 100 victories, including 11 Grand Slams, he inspired a whole generation to adopt the now indispensable VS. "What pleased me, and it does not normally happen, is that Babolat has remained a family business. I salute their 150 years of success and professionalism, something I was able to witness for myself when I visited Lyon and could observe the heart of production," adds Borg.

VS went on to embody a golden age, the symbol of victories for Arthur Ashe, Martina Navratilova, Jimmy Connors and Yannick Noah. Almost all of the game's champions lifted their trophies thanks to the natural gut strings, with each one hailing the technology's contribution. More than simply mentioning the comfort it brought to the game, many cite the characteristic sound of the gut and its ability to control and caress the ball. For all of them, the VS became an extension of their hand, and therefore impossible to disassociate from their triumphs.

WHAT PLEASED ME, AND IT DOES NOT NORMALLY HAPPEN, IS THAT BABOLAT HAS REMAINED A FAMILY BUSINESS. I SALUTE THEIR 150 YEARS OF SUCCESS.

— Björn Borg

ABOVE Björn Borg receives a golden VS from Paul Babolat.

OPPOSITE PAGE Björn Borg lifts the Wimbledon trophy for the second time, beating Jimmy Connors at the tournament's centenary in 1977.

FOLLOWING PAGES Arthur Ashe and Björn Borg arrive on court for their quarter-final match at Wimbledon on 2 July 1975.

DONNAY

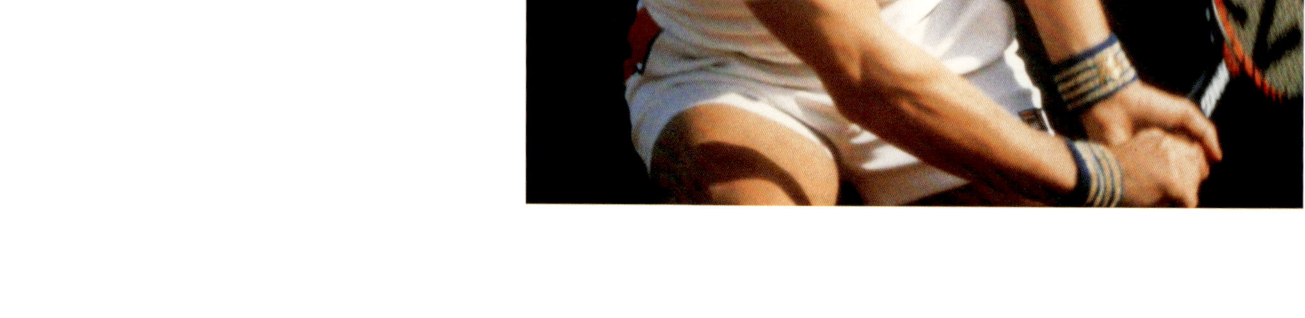

LEFT AND BELOW Björn Borg and the VS strings with which he won the tournament at Roland-Garros for the second time in his career.

OPPOSITE PAGE Björn Borg cannot contain his with jubilation after beating John McEnroe at the end of a legendary duel that revolutionised the history of tennis. This victory would be his last on the Wimbledon grass courts.

PAGE 69 VS appears in large letters on the strings of Björn Borg's racquet.

ALL MY LIFE
I HAVE PLAYED
WITH BABOLAT'S
NATURAL GUT STRINGS
IN MY RACQUETS AS
THEY ARE THE FINEST
QUALITY IN TERMS
OF EQUIPMENT.

— Björn Borg

BANCROFT

TOP Jan Kodeš faces Stan Smith in the semi-final of the men's singles on Wimbledon's Centre Court on 7 July 1972.

RIGHT Arthur Ashe also trusted the quality of VS strings. He was the first African-American player in world tennis's history to win Wimbledon in 1968 while still an amateur.

OPPOSITE PAGE Stan Smith facing Andrés Gimeno in the first match of the Davis Cup in 1972.

VS
rdes
ennis
BABOLAT
MAILLOT
WITT
VS

THE FIRST TIME I PLAYED USING VS STRINGS WAS ALSO THE FIRST TIME I BEAT MY MOTHER AT TENNIS. SOMETHING IT IS IMPOSSIBLE TO FORGET!

— Martina Navratilova

OPPOSITE PAGE Martina Navratilova at Roland–Garros in 1975, the tournament where she reached the final against American Chris Evert.

ABOVE Martina Navratilova makes her debut on the American circuit in 1973 aged 16.

LEFT Martina Navratilova wins her first Grand Slam singles title at Wimbledon in 1978 against Chris Evert, becoming No. 1 in the world rankings for the first time in her career.

1983

YANNICK NOAH WINS ROLAND–GARROS AGAINST MATS WILANDER

ABOVE AND RIGHT Yannick Noah enjoys his triumph at Roland–Garros having beaten Mats Wilander in the final on 5 June 1983.

OPPOSITE PAGE Yannick Noah celebrates his victory with his family in the stands. He became the fifth and last Frenchman to lift this trophy.

FOLLOWING PAGES Both players made the VS excel on all surfaces.

ROSSIGNOL
F200

J'espere que le "VS" participera à une victoire prochaine de la France dans une future Coupe Davis, et que comme Henri Cochet je pourrai me vanter d'avoir remporté ce merveilleux trophée grâce à vos garnitures

Amitiés sincères

Noah

ABOVE Yannick Noah with Paul Babolat visiting the factory where natural gut strings are made. During the visit he praised the outstanding qualities of the VS string in the vistors' book.

OPPOSITE PAGE On this drying rack are VS strings that will play their part in future successes.

PAGE 81 His 1985 triumph at Wimbledon meant 17-year-old Boris Becker became the youngest winner of the tournament.

I PLAYED FOR 17 YEARS AT THE HIGHEST LEVEL AND NEVER USED ANYTHING BUT BABOLAT'S NATURAL GUT DURING THE ENTIRE TIME. TO ME IT WAS A SOURCE OF PRIDE. I NEVER WANTED TO CHANGE, EVEN WHEN I WAS PLAYING ON CLAY WHEN SOMETIMES I WOULD BREAK MY STRINGS AFTER 20–25 MINUTES. TOO BAD, I COULD TAKE 10–12 RACQUETS IN MY BAG IF I HAD TO, BUT I NEVER PARTED WITH THEM. YOU NEVER CHANGE A WINNING TEAM! I HAVE ONE PARTICULAR MEMORY OF BABOLAT'S NATURAL GUT, THAT OF IT BEING 8.5 MM OR 125 MM IN DIAMETER, WHICH IS REALLY UNCONVENTIONAL. SOMETIMES I USED AN EVEN FINER GAUGE. I WON ALL MY WIMBLEDON TITLES WITH THIS STRING AND IT IS A MEMORY THAT WILL STAY WITH ME FOREVER AS REMAINING LOYAL TO BABOLAT WAS IMPORTANT TO ME.

— Boris Becker

1985

BOORIS BECKER BECOMES THE YOUNGEST PLAYER TO WIN WIMBLEDON AGED 17

THE BRAND'S SIGNATURE EVOLVES

By the end of the 1970s, VS was being displayed on the racquets of players around the world and notably at Wimbledon where Stan Smith won in 1972. Using the space available on the strings to imprint the VS brand had never been seen before. It was an idea so ingenious that it provoked a reaction from rival racquet manufacturers, who were envious they had not thought of it themselves, as they realised such a visible space was ideal. From then on, they too wanted to advertise by printing their logo in the centre of their racquets. Babolat let them to proceed without making a fuss, responding instead by changing their brand signature. 1986 saw the birth of the double line, which from now on was added at the base of the strings. These two lines were confirmation that whatever brand the racquet frame might be, its strings were made by Babolat. The VS logo would remain visible on its own for just three years.

OPPOSITE PAGE Stan Smith wins Wimbledon in 1972 beating Ilie Nastase after one of the greatest finals in the history of tennis.

ABOVE An advertisement for the double line, Babolat's new symbol on its racquet strings.

RIGHT The double line shares Pete Sampras's strings with the logo of his new racquet manufacturer.

BABOLAT NEVER STOPS INNOVATING

Both experienced and professional tennis players understand that their choice of strings is as important as their choice of racquet, since the strings are an integral part of a player's arsenal. It is essential, therefore, that stringing be done with care, as this adds to the overall quality of both the strings and the frame. If poorly inserted, strings can lose all their characteristics and so, keeping alive its tradition of innovation, Babolat launched "CORDYNEL," the first electric stringing machine. It was a major step forward for the industry as it was a formidable time-saving tool as well. Before this switch to electrification, it was necessary to rely on a punch and the strength of the stringer's arm, which inevitably limited what could be achieved. By mechanising and adding electronics, it was now possible to improve the quality of the finished article. Cording craftsmen could finally take advantage of a more sophisticated tool which also allowed the trade to become more professional. Nowadays these CORDYNEL machines are available in sports stores for amateur players as well as at selected professional tournaments. In the 1980s, Babolat once again showed itself ahead of the game by creating "Competition Team," assembling a group of expert stringers, who were exceptional racquet preparers and who followed players to tournaments to assist them. This on-site service guaranteed the quality of stringing necessary to meet the demands of the circuit. In 1992, this family firm, which Pierre Babolat had now taken over, continued to distinguish itself in the industry with the creation of synthetic multi-strand strings—VX—a state of the art invention that appealed to many players.

TOP Paul and Pierre Babolat are carrying on the work of their illustrious ancestors and continuing to innovate.

ABOVE Thanks to the Cordynel machine, racquet stringing has been modernised and can be done with greater precision.

OPPOSITE PAGE Babolat's first multifilament tennis strings.

This multifilament string, composed of nylon or polyamide fibres, is made by braiding together several filaments wrapped in one or more protective layers and is the closest type of string to one made of natural gut. It provides great comfort during play, as well as control and excellent ball speed, and players with weak forearms certainly prefer it. In fact, the multifilament also provides a certain level of shock-absorption that significantly cushions vibrations caused by shocks. Later Babolat continued to focus on every aspect of the game by setting up the RDC (Racquet Diagnostic Centre), a professional tool providing a complete assessment of the characteristics of a racquet and strings in less than two minutes. This machine is capable of calculating a wide range of information from the strength of the frame and the strings to inertia, balance or weight. Thanks to the RDC it became possible to customise racquets and monitor loss of tension in their strings.

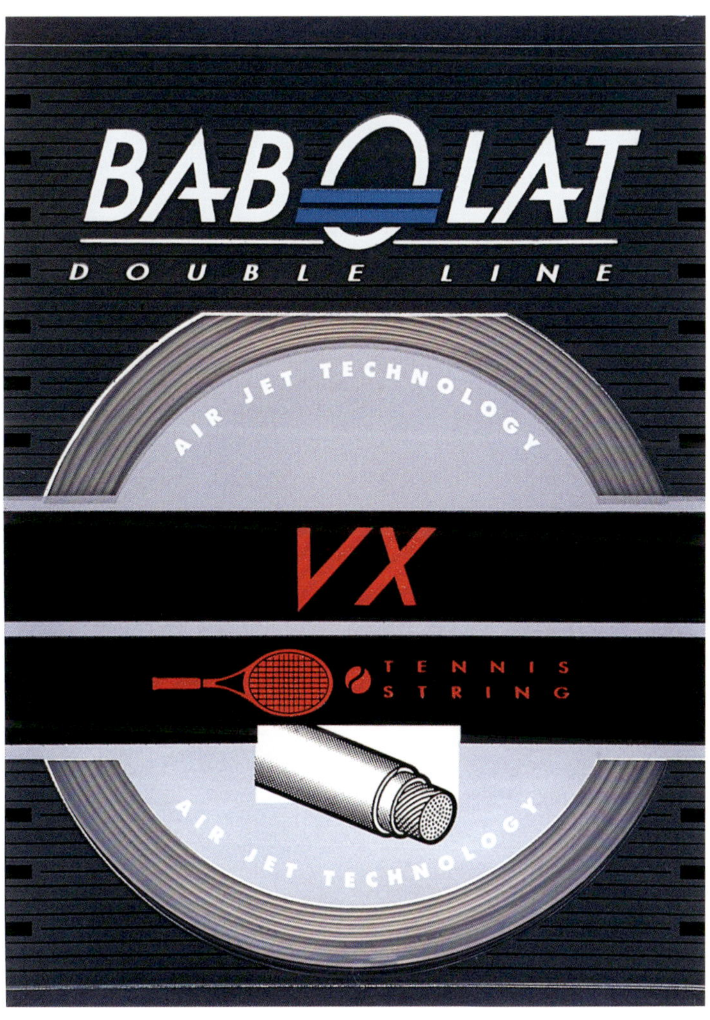

ELASTOCROSS, THE MAGIC INGREDIENT

Babolat conceived the idea of devising a tool that would extend string life and make repositioning strings easier and in 1982, the Elastocross was born. These small Polyamide pads, for insertion at the intersection of vertical and horizontal strings, were created to reduce friction and protect against the strings becoming prematurely worn and suddenly breaking. Players now got into the habit of fitting these crosspieces, which had no adverse effect either on the feel or balance of the racquet and with this seemingly simple tool, they could double the lifespan of their strings. Elastocross pads are inserted both before and during a match and have led to a number of superstitions. For some players, such as Pete Sampras, they became part of their routine for concentrating and the American champion, who won 14 Grand Slams, never removed his Elastocross, replacing them over and over again during games. Later on, Alex Corretja developped the habit of storing Elastocross in one of his socks to use during a match.

THE CRAFT OF RACQUET STRINGING — LUCIEN NOGUÈS

"A badly strung racquet is like a Ferrari with a 4L engine," is the favourite saying of Lucien Noguès, one of Babolat's most iconic racquet stringers. After 43 years spent in the company of the greatest champions, he has not lost one iota of his passion. For him, it all began in September 1981 when Paul Babolat had just launched the company's competition service and Lucien landed his dream job. He was to tour tournaments in an 8-metre American Dodge van, customised for Babolat VS, to offer his invaluable expertise to the professional players of the day. Inside was a television, video recorder, sofa, refrigerator and racquet stringing machines. "On the motorway between Madrid and Barcelona en route to my second tournament, I lost both rear wheels on the van so my entreprise could have ended right there," he recalls with amusement. Instead, Lucien would spend more than 300 nights each year in hotels. When he started out, tennis racquets were made of wood with natural gut strings the most popular. Whether Björn Borg, Yannick Noah, Jimmy Connors, Eddie Dips, Tomas Schmid or Manuel Orantes, "at that time, the players used two racquets for each tournament and broke very few," says Lucien. "Spin was practically non-existent as it was the era of slice and 'chip and charge'." At the time, natural gut was considered the most effective and precise string. However, it had a few drawbacks, moisture being the principal one. "You couldn't leave your racquet sitting by your damp socks, as the slightest drop made a difference."

Björn Borg, the greatest champion of his era, went through a lot of gut. He played with very thin, unvarnished strings and required very high tension of around 34–35kg. "Their sound was phenomenal but at night he'd be woken up by the crack of his racquet strings snapping." It was a golden era. Tennis was all the rage and every racquet passed through the hands of the competition service department.

AT THAT TIME THE PLAYERS USED TWO RACQUETS FOR EACH TOURNAMENT AND BROKE VERY FEW. THE SPIN WAS PRACTICALLY NON-EXISTENT AS IT WAS THE ERA OF SLICES AND "CHIP AND CHARGE".

— Lucien Noguès

OPPOSITE PAGE Lucien Noguès, a member of "Team Compétition" has strung the racquets of the greatest champions.

LEFT Yannick Noah at the Australian Open in 1990.

ABOVE Jimmy Connors at Wimbledon in 1984.

RECENTLY, I WAS LUCKY ENOUGH TO HAVE THE CHANCE OF VISITING THE LYON FACTORY WHERE I WAS ABLE TO SEE LUCIEN NOGUÈS, THEIR ICONIC RACQUET STRINGER, AGAIN. HE HAS ALWAYS BEEN VERY AMUSING AND KIND AND IT WAS TOUCHING TO SEE THAT HE STILL PLAYS A MAJOR PART WITHIN THE BRAND.

— Boris Becker

In 1983 Yannick Noah defeated Mats Wilander to win the French Open, both using racquets with Babolat strings. Noah played with fairly low tension springs suited to large wooden racquets. "If he came to see us during the first few days of a tournament and didn't change his tension, we knew he would go all the way. When he started tampering with his tension, we could almost smell a plane ticket in his pocket!" says Lucien. When the hybrid string was introduced, it became possible to give the ball more spin but it also meant extra work for the stringers. Unlike gut, a hybrid string loses tension when static (without being played) so has to be changed more often and sometimes it's necessary to improvise. "Synthetic strings do not like extreme conditions at all. During a match in Frējus between France and Sweden, Kent Carlsson asked us to string his racquets quite tight. They were then stored in sealed plastic bags with drinks in a cool box to avoid losing tension. However, when they were once again exposed to outside heat, the frames and strings expanded and a string could break without the racquet being played."

The workload has therefore changed over the years as have the techniques. Electronics have become part of the equation and the time required for stringing has dropped. It used to take more than 30 minutes to string a wooden racquet, now it takes between 15 and 17 minutes. As for the players themselves, they need more equipment. "At the start of a tournament, it often resembles a war zone. To begin with, each stringer will have 30 or 40 frames to prepare per day. Some players need as many as ten racquets per match." To begin with the competition support team numbered 6 stringers, now that figure is twenty and they are on call from 6am to 2am. "You have to know how to live as a pack since we work, eat and sleep together. But, above all, you have to maintain the same high standard from the first racquet to the last." With more than 650 tournaments to his credit, Lucien Nogues' career spans continents and changing times and he has seen many champions come and go. While the needs of players, strings and materials have all evolved, the racquet remains an extension of their arm and all players have an acute memory of how that feels, bordering on an obsession. "Boris Becker was able to detect a difference of 3–5g between two racquets," he explains, "so we have to find a common language to decipher players' sensations. They go to the stringer in the same way as they go to the doctor and they often repeat that the racquet 'is not going anywhere'. It is our job to understand what they actually mean. The strings are the racquet's motor, making us a bit like their track engineer." Since 1981 Babolat and its Research and Development Department have been developing prototypes based on the evidence of all these players. Tested and retested, these prototypes have led to major advances in modern tennis. "I drove everyone crazy in my quest to get answers, but I have so many happy memories. From a technical point of view, I am first and foremost happy to have been able to make a contribution to the development of this sport. It's still called 'playing' tennis, so let's keep making the toys!" concludes Lucien cheerfully.

THEY GO TO THE STRINGER IN THE SAME WAY AS THEY GO TO THE DOCTOR AND THEY OFTEN REPEAT THAT THE RACQUET "IS NOT GOING ANYWHERE." IT IS OUR JOB TO UNDERSTAND WHAT THEY ACTUALLY MEAN. THE STRINGS ARE THE RACQUET'S MOTOR, MAKING US A BIT LIKE THEIR TRACK ENGINEER.

— Lucien Noguès

JEAN–JACQUES POUPON, THE STRINGER OF CHAMPIONS AND THE CHAMPION STRINGER

He set up his own workshop, measuring some 20 square metres, at his home in Concarneau, Brittany, and it was there that he created his own masterpieces by preparing the racquets of the greatest champions with a goldsmith's precision. Attention to detail was his cardinal virtue, he kept his passion for his craft right to the end. In just a few years, Jean–Jacques Poupon became a leading figure in French tennis. As a racquet stringer for the French national teams, he wore a tricolour tracksuit on court just like the players. It was a revolutionary move, led by Yannick Noah in 1991 who, as captain of *Les Bleus*, argued that the stringer is not simply a technician, but a fully–fledged team member. Jean–Jacques Poupon became the attentive ear and faithful advisor to many generations of players. He witnessed Yannick Noah's triumphs in 1983 and went on to help guide Amélie Mauresmo to the top. He was both father and big brother to Richard Gasquet and Jo–Wilfried Tsonga, and Rafael Nadal adored him. In addition to his work with the French national team, he regularly officiated at Babolat. For some twenty years, he exported his talent to the four corners of the globe and was always hailed for his professionalism. After his passing in 2024, he left behind a huge legacy and an indelible mark on the world of tennis.

OPPOSITE PAGE Boris Becker, seen here at the 1989 US Open, could not do without Babolat strings.

LEFT Kent Carlsson in 1987.

ABOVE Jean–Jacques Poupon, the legendary stringer for the French teams.

MOYA

THE FIRST RACQUET

1994

2004

1994 MARKED A MAJOR TURNING POINT FOR THE COMPANY. AFTER MORE THAN A CENTURY DEDICATED TO STRINGS AND ACCESSORIES, BABOLAT LAUNCHED ITS VERY FIRST RANGE OF TENNIS RACQUET FRAMES. IT WAS MORE THAN SIMPLY A CHALLENGE, IT WAS A MAJOR GAMBLE THAT PIERRE BABOLAT DARED TO TAKE AS THE CIRCUMSTANCES WERE NOT VERY FAVOURABLE.

On 8 June 1998, Carlos Moya, overcome with emotion, collapsed on the clay court at Roland–Garros where he had just won his first championship by beating his friend Àlex Corretja. His white polo shirt was smeared with ochre and, unable to hold back his tears, he hurled his light blue racquet into the stands in celebration of the greatest moment of his career. Among the crowd at the Philippe–Chatrier Court, where the men's singles final is traditionally held every year on the last Sunday of the tournament, was Pierre Babolat, who particularly savoured the victory. This success marked the beginning of his collection of Grand Slam trophies won with a Babolat racquet. As Pelé, the legendary football player was presenting the Musketeers trophy to the 22–year–old player, Pierre knew that his gamble had paid off. Several dreams came true that day.

Four years earlier, the risk he had taken seemed crazy. To start making tennis racquets at a time when the market was in crisis, you had to be pretty forward thinking. At the time, tennis was no longer really fashionable and racquet

OPENING AND OPPOSITE PAGE In 1998 at Roland–Garros, Carlos Moya becomes the first player to win a Grand Slam with a Babolat racquet, beating his countryman, Àlex Corretja, who also played using Babolat strings.

sales were plummeting, leading to some manufacturers sadly being forced to close down. Even internally, teeth were grinding and few people believed in it. Except Pierre Babolat, of course, who wanted to diversify the brand. He came up with an innovative idea, that of offering players a single price of 890 French francs and a limited choice of racquets. Three frame profiles were then available instore, offering the choice of control, power or all-round performance. There was something for every type of player. Experienced players opted for the Pure range, while those who played less often, chose the Soft range. Colours were basic—blue, red and grey—while the Babolat logo, the characteristic double line that had previously been on the strings, was recycled and appeared on the frame.

Starting to make racquets meant your former partners, the people with whom you had worked with for years making strings, were now your competitors, going from allies to rivals, which was quite an about turn. Fortunately, at the start of this new venture, nobody was very concerned about this latest entrant into the market. Babolat had yet to be taken seriously and the competition paid them little attention, which allowed the brand to evolve in its own time.

"We grew at a snail's pace. The world was going through profound change and our competitors were too focused on their own problems to take us seriously," says Éric Babolat. Slowly but surely, Babolat improved, becoming a contender to be reckoned with. All that remained was to find its first racquet ambassador, someone who would lead the way and encourage players to buy Babolat.

WE GREW AT A SNAIL'S PACE. THE WORLD WAS GOING THROUGH PROFOUND CHANGE AND OUR COMPETITORS WERE TOO FOCUSED ON THEIR OWN PROBLEMS TO TAKE US SERIOUSLY.

— Éric Babolat

ABOVE Éric Babolat has taken over the family business and has continued to successfully develop its racquets.

OPPOSITE PAGE Power, Drive, Control. Babolat's first range of tennis racquets is launched in 1994 and stands out for its segmented offer.

1994

LAUNCH OF BABOLAT'S FIRST RANGE OF TENNIS RACQUETS

THE SEARCH FOR AN AMBASSADOR

The search was no easy task given the DNA of a professional tennis player, who is hard-wired to his rituals and has a close personal, almost reverential relationship with his equipment. The company tried hard to convince Tim Henman or even Arnaud Boetsch, players who already used Babolat strings, but neither was bold enough to take the plunge. A racquet is a work tool, an extension of the arm and sometimes impossible to separate from a player's body. Courage is needed to disrupt such well-established habits, especially if you are already a winner. "When players were blind-testing all-black racquets, our frames were popular but, as soon as we added our logo, the other leading brands were preferred for their track record,' explains Babolat's CEO.

So, instead of concentrating on the stars of the circuit, up-and-coming young players were targeted. Among them were Fernando González and the Belgian Kim Clijsters, who signed with Babolat at the age of fifteen. Carlos Moya, who was twenty when he tried out Babolat frames for the first time in 1996 says: "I remember feeling immediately that this racquet could offer me something new but I hesitated since, at the time, I was still playing with another brand. However, it was only a few months later, at the end of the season, that I tested the racquet at the Bercy tournament." During the course of that week at the Palais Omnisports de Paris-Bercy, equipped with just two Pure Drive blue framed racquets, he beat Tim Henman in the first round before pulling off a stunning victory against Boris Becker, the defending champion at the time. In an atmosphere that was electric, he reached the quarter-finals, thereby achieving the greatest result of his fledgling career. Quite something when you consider Bercy was only supposed to be a test for the racquet under 'real' conditions! As a result, Moya's unexpected success finally made his mind up and he adopted Babolat permanently. "That racquet was a no-brainer! A few weeks later I reached the Australian Open final and my career took off," he says. It was ironic that Carlos Moya had let himself be swayed by a racquet that was far below competition standards and one generally recommended for women beginners. "It was like giving a town car to a rally driver," explains Éric Babolat. It weighed 270 grams, whereas professional players used much heavier control racquets, weighing around 350 grams. Moya had been looking for a powerful racquet that moved quickly through the air. "It was explained to me that this was a women's model but pro players only need a couple of minutes to know if a racquet is right for them and that's how I felt. Pure Drive changed my career," adds the man who became World No. 1 two years later. After his Australian final against Pete Sampras in 1997, the media exploded. Everyone went crazy for this new generation Spaniard, with his long hair, short sleeves and flamboyant game. Moya stood out as he played from the front with an open stance forehand, and also because he had this unusual racquet. His crowning moment came in 1998, when he won at Monte-Carlo and then, on a Sunday in June, at Roland-Garros. Carlos Moya remains the first player to have provided Babolat with a major success thanks to a racquet. With a Grand Slam title, the brand was propelled to the top and that unforgettable victory on the Paris

ABOVE In 1998, the day after Carlos Moya wins at Roland-Garros, Babolat racquets are officially launched at the Gerry Weber Open in Germany.

IT WAS EXPLAINED TO ME THAT THIS WAS A WOMEN'S MODEL BUT PRO PLAYERS ONLY NEED A COUPLE OF MINUTES TO KNOW IF A RACQUET IS RIGHT FOR THEM AND THAT'S HOW I FELT. PURE DRIVE CHANGED MY CAREER.

— Carlos Moya

clay court validated absolutely everything, from the moments of doubt to the daring gamble and the controversial choices. This dedication on court was the ultimate proof that Babolat was a reliable manufacturer in the racquet market and the future promised to be a triumphant one. In the same year, Kim Clijsters and Fernando Gonzalez, both spotted by Babolat at the age of twelve, also won in their junior categories. In 1998, the huge amount of publicity this generated marked the beginning of a love affair with the brand. On the circuit, Àlex Corretja, Li Na and Andy Roddick signed with the French company, even though the racquet was not yet on sale in the United States. But in the midst of this success, tragedy struck the Babolat family, as just two months after revelling in the triumph of Carlos Moya at Roland-Garros, Pierre Babolat, the company's visionary CEO, was killed in a plane crash on his way back from the US Open. "I immediately picked up the company torch, to which I was deeply attached, and we all pulled together to continue the work," explains Éric Babolat, Pierre's son, who is determined to carry on the great family legacy of innovation and achievement.

ABOVE Carlos Moya triumphs playing with the Pure Drive, the racquet that will remain with him throughout his career.

PAGE 99 In 1997, a few months after adopting the Pure Drive, Carlos Moya reaches the final of the Australian Open in Melbourne.

THAT RACQUET WAS A NO—BRAINER! A FEW WEEKS LATER I REACHED THE AUSTRALIAN OPEN FINAL AND MY CAREER TOOK OFF.

— Carlos Moya

KIM CLIJSTERS

The Belgian player has never been separated from her Pure Drive, adopting it at the beginning of her career. The loyal racquet took her to the top of the world rankings.

Adecco

ANDY RODDICK

With his aggressive style of play, the American has long placed his trust in Babolat. Using his Pure Drive, a true extension of his arm, the speed of his service was clocked at 249.4 km/hour.

1998

CARLOS MOYA WINS ROLAND–GARROS

Madrid, 16 November 2010

To my dear friends at Babolat

I am writing this letter as I wanted to tell you personally of my decision to quit professional tennis. I intend to announce this at a press conference in Madrid on Wednesday 17 November.

My last competition will be the Seville Masters at the beginning of December. These past years have been the best years of my life so far, full of good times—and some that were not so good—but, without doubt, I will always keep the happy memories in my heart.

We have been together since 1997 and, in my second tournament with Babolat, I reached the final of the Australian Open, a tournament that truly changed my life. I can still recall the first time I tried one of your racquets and, looking back today, it amuses me to admit that many of my friends teased me because I was playing with a Babolat. But I was confident my decision was the right one and time has proved that. Today, Babolat is one of the most respected and recognised brands of tennis racquets in the world. Even though I don't know most of you personally, I really want to thank you for your work behind the scenes and to share every one of my victories with you.

I have now embarked on a new life which I am certain will be even more fantastic as I am the proud father of a 3-month-old little girl. It will not be easy and this time I won't be able to rely on your support, but I will do my best and I will certainly stay involved in tennis and sport in general because that is what has given me everything I have today.

Once again, thank you very much.

I wish you all the best.

— Carlos Moya

OPPOSITE PAGE The Musketeers Cup is won by Carlos Moya at Roland-Garros in 1998.

THE PURE DRIVE — 30 YEARS OF A LEGENDARY RACQUET

"As soon as my coach took it out of its plastic wrapping, I knew it was the one. It was love at first sight and I could see it would become an extension of my arm." When Kim Clijsters describes her first encounter with Pure Drive at the age of fifteen, it is as though she is describing a lover. The Belgian player never parted company with the blue racquet that accompanied her to the very top of world tennis. With it, Kim Clijsters added four Grand Slam trophies, won in Australia and at the US Open, for the Babolat cupboard and, for the past thirty years, Pure Drive has inspired similar love stories. "Have you noticed how beautiful it is? I put an orange grip on the handle as it looks awesome with the blue. I'm so attached to it, I even find it hard lending it to my husband," says Flora Birnbaum, Technical Director of the Bagneux tennis club. It is looked after like a jewel, pampered as though it were the most precious of instruments. This deep blue racquet has won the hearts of so many players, pros, top coaches and those who only play on Sundays, and spend as much time drinking coffee as they do on court playing. Over the course of three decades, it has become the world's best-selling racquet, the must-have item in every player's locker. But why has it been such a success? The general consensus is that it is aesthetically pleasing and has universal appeal. When you play tennis, you are repeating the strokes lost in your own private world, as you image winning the most prestigious trophies and dreaming of holding the same racquet as your idol. Do you get the picture? With Pure Drive, that vision becomes a reality. For the first time ever, an amateur player can progress using the same frame as their favourite champion. However, when this model first appeared in 1994 it was primarily aimed at beginners, who either lacked technique or were looking for power. At that time the racquet was unusual in that it was light and rigid, had a streamlined frame and a very different colour scheme. Above all, though, Pure Drive was all about making life easier and playing well. It was every frustrated player's dream. "It's closer to being a Porsche than a Ferrari as you don't have to be a great driver to get the best out of it," explains Éric Babolat. Its light weight actually makes it very easy to handle and some players choose it more for how it feels when volleying than for its baseline power. As it evolved, the racquet would come to suit all styles from that of very powerful players to those whose game was largely based on counter attacking, with the frame providing the necessary ferocity to overcome their opponents. In terms of popularity, Carlos Moya's win at the French Open accelerated everything and his Grand Slam success marked the beginning of an epic story. After him, other champions adopted the racquet and sales took off around the world. Using Pure Drive, Andy Roddick broke the service speed record, clocking 247 km/hour thanks to this 'weapon'. It was Garbiñe Muguruza who triumphed in style at Roland-Garros and Wimbledon, Sofia Kenin in Australia and Fabio Fognini with his nonchalant style of play. But it is also Jennifer who plays her first "match" at the back of the court behind her more experienced partner or Henry who plays doubles every Sunday morning with his friends. Pure drive belongs to everyone and has done so for over thirty years.

ABOVE Kim Clijsters and Li Na face each other in the final of the Australian Open, both playing with Pure Drive.

OPPOSITE PAGE Garbiñe Muguruza, playing with her Pure Drive, distinguishes herself at the 2016 French Open at Roland-Garros by beating Serena Williams.

FOLLOWING PAGES Sofia Kenin is victorious at the 2020 Australian Open.

CUTTING-EDGE TECHNOLOGIES IN SUPPORT OF CHANGE

For over thirty years, Babolat has been constantly developing its flagship product to bring ever more stability to its frame, drawing inspiration notably from the findings of the aerospace industry. While preserving its DNA, twelve generations of Pure Drive have been created since the first was launched in 1994. Even when a shot is not centered, the racquet's HTR (High Torsional Rigidity) system allows a higher return of energy and a sudden explosion when the ball leaves the racquet. To improve the feel and reduce the vibrations caused when hitting the ball, SMACWRAP technology is used. A viscoelastic material incorporated into the framework of the racquet allows the player to deaden the noise and vibrations, so that only those related to the sensation of the ball are felt. Potentially harmful vibrations that can cause problems for the tendons in the arm are minimised. The result is the player achieves better "touch" and experiences less trauma.

Babolat
PURE DRIVE
Babolat
Babolat
FRAME STRING INTERACTION
FSI
TEAM
BABOLAT
BABOLAT

THE PURE DRIVE RANGE OF PRODUCTS

Alongside the racquet is a range of dedicated accessories, including bags, clothing (t-shirts, caps) and the Propulse Fury shoe, which is the same shade of deep blue as the Pure Drive. In the same collection, two distinctive blue strings are also available—the RPM Power and Touch VS—that make it possible to get the most out of the Pure Drive frame.

ABOVE The Pure Drive has become the top-selling racquet in the world.

OPPOSITE PAGE Babolat expands by launching its first range of tennis balls in 2001.

Babolat
TEAM
TM
Babolat TM

BABOLAT & MICHELIN, A UNIQUE PARTNERSHIP

Sudden braking, sliding, skidding or sharp acceleration, a tennis player's movements can sometimes mimic those of a racing car, without the fierce roar of the engine. As with car tyres, the sole of the player's shoe is the only thing in contact with the ground, so it is essential this ensures the best road grip possible. In 2002, when Babolat decided to launch its first ever range of shoes, the brand simply turned to the world's number one tyre manufacturer, Michelin and its iconic Bibendum. "We needed their expertise as regards contact with the ground, in this case between the road and the tyre. We realised that beyond the racquet a player needed to be able to move around easily," explains Éric Babolat, "and, when it came to playing tennis, there was very little choice of shoe on the market." Their collaboration with Michelin was no small thing. The two brands both wanted to make an impression by creating the ideal shoe for racquet sports. If you study a player's movements during a match, you soon realise that 80% of their movements are actually lateral, whereas most sports shoes at that time were only designed for running backwards and forwards in. If this was a leap into the unknown for two companies that had never before made shoes, it was also an ideal opportunity for creativity and innovation. In addition to its brand image, Michelin also brought its exceptional technological expertise. It would take two years of research at its technology centre to develop the perfect sole. This meant a rubber sole that ensured good resistance against abrasion and would act as a shock absorber for the foot. As with high performance tyres, a clearly defined tread pattern was created that combined different criteria. The inner surface of the sole looked like a conventional tyre, which helped to improve grip, while around it there were thin strips designed to control sliding. This initial sole could be adapted to all types of court. After this, specific models would be designed according to the surface being played on, whether hard, clay, grass or indoors. "We work on the contour of the surface according to the movements of the foot to give the greatest ease and best grip possible in the right place at the right time," explains Marion Cornu, marketing director for tennis. This partnership between Babolat and Michelin resulted in dedicated models produced for different playing surfaces for tennis, badminton and padel. Andy Roddick quickly began wearing these shoes, as did Félix Auger-Aliassime while progressing as a junior. Babolat also supplied many coaches in clubs. Ten years later, in addition to Michelin, Babolat went into partnership with textile manufacturer Chamatex to improve the upper end of its shoe range, creating ultra-light shoes for tennis and padel.

WE NEEDED THEIR EXPERTISE AS REGARDS CONTACT WITH THE GROUND, IN THIS CASE BETWEEN THE ROAD AND THE TYRE. WE REALISED THAT BEYOND THE RACQUET A PLAYER NEEDED TO BE ABLE TO MOVE AROUND EASILY AND, WHEN IT CAME TO PLAYING TENNIS, THERE WAS VERY LITTLE CHOICE OF SHOE ON THE MARKET.

— Éric Babolat

WE WORK ON THE CONTOUR OF THE SURFACE ACCORDING TO THE MOVEMENTS OF THE FOOT TO GIVE THE GREATEST EASE AND BEST GRIP POSSIBLE IN THE RIGHT PLACE AT THE RIGHT TIME.

— Marion Cornu

OPPOSITE PAGE In 2002, the first Babolat tennis shoe appears on the market, developed in partnership with Michelin.

ABOVE Andy Roddick, who became one of the company's first ambassadors, immediately adopted this shoe that had been specially designed for playing tennis.

NADAL

THE THUNDERBOLT

2004

2024

2005

RAFAEL NADAL WINS HIS FIRST ROLAND–GARROS TITLE

HOW DO YOU EXPLAIN THE EXTRAORDINARY OR SUM UP A CAREER SPANNING MORE THAN TWENTY YEARS WHEN SO OFTEN THAT CAREER HAS BEEN NOTHING SHORT OF SUBLIME? BY WINNING TWENTY–FOUR GRAND SLAMS AND REMAINING WITH THE SAME BRAND HE HAS USED SINCE HE WAS EIGHT–YEAR–OLD, RAFAEL NADAL HAS SWEPT BABOLAT TO UNDREAMED OF HEIGHTS. SAYING GOODBYE TO HIM IS LIKE WAIVING FAREWELL TO THE HERO OF A FAIRY TALE. IT IS TO SALUTE HIS SUPERSTITIONS THAT SOMETIMES BORDERED ON OBSESSIONS, SUCH AS POSITIONING BOTTLES BY HIM WITH MILLIMETRE PRECISION WHEN SITTING ON COURT. THERE WERE ALL THE LINES HE PAINSTAKINGLY STEPPED OVER AND THE WAY HE METHODICALLY ADJUSTED HIS SHORTS EACH TIME BEFORE HE SERVED. ALONGSIDE ALL THESE RITUALS, THERE WAS, MOST IMPORTANTLY, HIS PINK, YELLOW AND BLACK RACQUET THAT WAS BEHIND ALL HIS SUCCESSES.

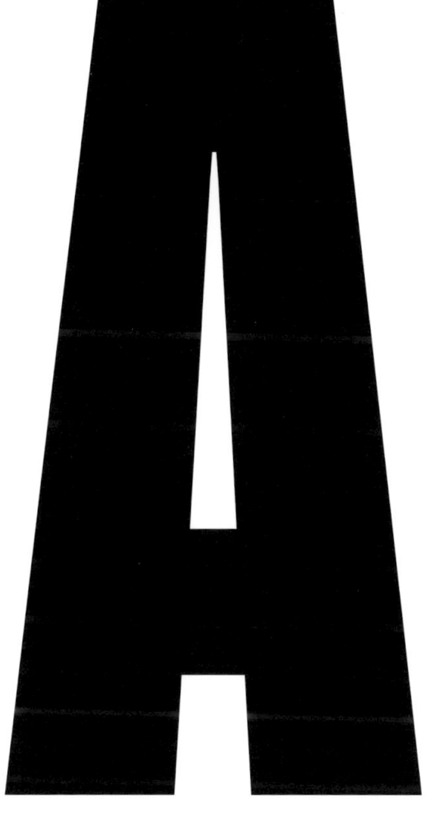

Amidst his rituals and at the very heart of his victories lies his faithful ally, the racquet he was so devoted to, just as a musician bonds with his instrument. The Pure Aero has played many symphonies and few wrong notes during the course of his life. Always respected when things went wrong and, above all, never a collateral victim, Rafael Nadal did not break a single racquet during his entire career. The model was destined for him and he never doubted it. From his early years, this tool has made him an exemplary champion, one that, in equal measure, has dismayed his opponents and won the admiration of his peers. "The racquet plays a vital part in any player's career, it's an extension of our arm and we experience every sensation through it. At the end of the day, if what you are feeling is not good, it is very difficult to achieve success," explains the young retiree.

OPENING Nadal at the Australian Open in Melbourne in 2020.

OPPOSITE PAGE Rafael Nadal during the 2015 French Open at Roland–Garros.

HOW THEY MET

The paths of Babolat and Rafa might never have crossed as tennis and Rafa could have bypassed each other completely. In Mallorca, where he was born and grew up, the young Nadal toyed with football, a sport he excelled at. He thought about it seriously, dreaming of following in the footsteps of his uncle Miguel Angel, an inspiring former player with FC Barcelona and the Spanish national team. But he was a homebody and the love of his family got the better of his ambition, so he chose tennis, his family and his island, rather than football, saying "no" to the training centre in Barcelona. Henceforth, Toni Nadal, Miguel Angel's brother, took charge of his nephew's sporting career and education. A tennis teacher, who acted as both guide and ally, it was he who discovered the Pure Drive in a shop in Manacor in 1994 and put it into Rafa's hand. At the time he was eight years old and that's how the Babolat story began, following a gift from his uncle and first mentor, who turned the right-handed Rafa to a left-hander on court. He achieved his first successes with this light, powerful racquet and the Balearic Islands champion was soon making a name for himself beyond the shores of his native archipelago. In the world of tennis, people began praising this young, dark-haired player who had boundless energy and, in the Babolat offices, things started moving. Willie Gomez, Babolat's sales representative for the south of Spain, was blown away by his talent and his fighting spirit. He used a powerful argument to convince him to join the brand: by signing with them, the young Rafa would be a bit closer to Carlos Moya, the newly crowned star of the day after his victory at Roland-Garros. Delighted to be playing with the same kind of racquet as his idol, Nadal permanently adopted the Pure Drive, signing his first junior contract at the age of twelve. Soon, his record of achievements was boosted by a series of very promising wins at the Open Super 12 at Auray in 1998, and then the Petits As de Tarbes in 2000, two prestigious international tournaments that gave a glimpse into what the future of tennis promised. The partnership moved to a new dimension in 2001 when an international contract was signed. As Jean-Christophe Verborg, Babolat's Competition Director, explains: "We developed our racquets a lot, taking into account his spin-focused game, but not just that, also his atypical body language at the time."

TOP Carlos Moya, with Éric Babolat, Nicolás Lapentti and Karim Alami, signing autographs at the official launch in April 1999 of the Woofer, the first interactive racquet, in Monte-Carlo.

ABOVE The young, 13-year-old, Rafael Nadal signing autographs after winning the Les Petits As tournament at Tarbes in 2000.

OPPOSITE PAGE Rafael Nadal wins the Les Petits As in 2000, a tournament from which many up-and-coming young players have emerged, among them Babolat champion Kim Clijsters.

A CUSTOM–MADE RACQUET

Rafa's obsession with spin and his lasso–style forehands became his trademark as he moved up to the senior ranks, where play is longer and faster. He adapted and began to gain valuable time on his opponents thanks to his body language. Before him, spin was not widely used as an attacking shot and, in the 1990s, the majority on court played flat. His unique game inspired Babolat to design a new frame with never–before–seen features, a racquet developed especially for him. In 2003, the Aeropro Drive was born, a precursor to the Pure Aero, a very flat racquet whose aerodynamic design encouraged rotation of the ball. It also allowed the racquet to penetrate the air more easily and had a smaller frame shape that enabled plenty of spin on both forehand and backhand shots, as well as speed. This new racquet was offered to Rafa in November 2004 in Manacor, where the Babolat teams had moved. While the Spaniard was initially reluctant to change, on that particular day he allowed himself to be convinced. Perfect, and above all focused on the sensations he experienced, he quickly adopted the new model after training. Equipped with a new fluorescent yellow frame, which suited his style perfectly, a month later he announced its arrival to the world during a weekend in Andalusia. Spain was facing the United States in the final of the Davis Cup and Rafael Nadal, just 18 years old, was part of the Spanish team alongside Carlos Moya and Juan Carlos Ferrero. On the advice of Moya, who had taken the young Majorcan player under his wing on the professional circuit, team captain, Jordi Arrese, selected Nadal, at that time ranked 50th in the world, to replace Ferrero in the singles and face the American champion Andy Roddick, the world No. 2. In front of 27,000 spellbound spectators in the Seville arena, Rafa pulled off one of the greatest results of his fledgling career by winning the match in four sets. "We had invited our American sales boss to introduce him to this young Spaniard who was playing with a Pure Aero," recalls Éric Babolat. "He was sceptical at first, wanting to know, 'who is this Nadal?' but, by the end of the weekend, all he could talk about was 'Rafa, Rafa, Rafa'!" While it was still too early to fully appreciate the full extent of the Nadal phenomenon, Rafa was beginning to create his own legend. A few months later, wearing long, baggy shorts, a vivid green sleeveless top and with a Babolat racquet, he was presented with his very first Grand Slam trophy by Zinedine Zidane at Roland–Garros, the first time he had entered. He was only nineteen and the company, itself still a young player in the market, now had a dream ambassador to promote its new racquet. Young and cool, he perfectly embodied the values of the Lyon–based firm. Like many people, Babolat had no idea at the time that this talented Spaniard would go on to earn a permanent place among the legends of the game, winning the French Open Grand Slam at Roland–Garros fourteen times.

OPPOSITE PAGE The Spaniard very quickly opted for the Pure Aero model, which favours spin.

RIGHT On 5 June 2005, Rafael Nadal wins the French Open at Roland–Garros on his first appearance at the tournament.

Babolat
aeropro
DRIVE
Babolat

WE HAD INVITED OUR AMERICAN SALES BOSS TO INTRODUCE HIM TO THIS YOUNG SPANIARD WHO WAS PLAYING WITH A PURE AERO. HE WAS SCEPTICAL AT FIRST, WANTING TO KNOW, "WHO IS THIS NADAL?" BUT, BY THE END OF THE WEEKEND, ALL HE COULD TALK ABOUT WAS "RAFA, RAFA, RAFA!"

— Éric Babolat

OPPOSITE PAGE Aero Pro Drive, the forerunner of the Pure Aero.

TOP Rafael Nadal, who was barely 18 years old at the time, beats Andy Roddick in front of a Spanish crowd in the final of the 2004 Davis Cup in Seville.

ABOVE Carlos Moya and Rafael Nadal emerge from training during the Davis Cup.

ALWAYS EXEMPLARY

Four years after making his professional debut, Nadal had already attained superstar status, driving fans, statistics and, inevitably, sponsors into a frenzy. But as the sirens of competing sponsors grew ever louder, he chose to stay put. Babolat had made every effort to keep its champion and he signed a ten-year contract with them, a first in the family's history. "I felt close to Babolat as to me it didn't seem like a company. For me, it was—and still is—first and foremost a family," he says. "Today, it's being run by the fifth generation and to me that matters." The brand has been as much a part of his 'clan' as his family. The close relationship between Nadal and Babolat has been one based on trust. His parents, Sebastian and Ana Maria, his sister, Maria Isabel, and his uncle Toni have all been part of his journey from the start. "Thanks to them, he always remained his natural self," explains Éric Babolat. "He says 'hello' and 'thank you' and is very warm, very tactile. Staying normal is all a part of his upbringing." In discussions with him and his requests, his dealings with Rafael Nadal always went very smoothly. Throughout the year, competition teams would travel with him and encourage him, when required, to test new products. While he never hesitated to provide regular feedback on his equipment, his requests always remained quite simple—to give him more spin and extra power. But, like any champion, Rafa wasn't really a fan of change. "If I tried another racquet, to begin with I didn't feel comfortable, while, with my racquet, I was relaxed as I knew it perfectly," explains Nadal. "I knew where to hit, I knew what I could do and, at any given moment, I knew how the ball would react to the way I moved." While his racquet did not change, small adjustments to enhance his strengths were regularly made. It is detailed work that requires long-term

I FELT CLOSE TO BABOLAT AS TO MS IT DIDN'T SEEM LIKE A COMPANY. FOR ME, IT WAS—AND STILL IS—FIRST AND FOREMOST A FAMILY. TODAY, IT'S BEING RUN BY THE FIFTH GENERATION AND TO ME THAT MATTERS.

— Rafael Nadal

RIGHT Rafael Nadal has always remained loyal to Babolat.

OPPOSITE PAGE Rafael Nadal arrives on Centre Court at Wimbledon in 2011 prior to his match against the American Michael Russell.

monitoring and, for this reason, at the end of each season, the Babolat teams visited Rafa in the calm environment of his island home at Manacor, away from prying eyes, cameras or microphones. Nadal welcomed them warmly and his unpretentiousness and kindness still surprises them. "He and his team routinely thanked us," confirms Jean-Christophe Verborg. "But that's what Rafa has always been about, from birthday messages to gifts for our children, when, without doubt, he must have had other things to think about." At work, too, he remained exemplary. While he is attached to his habits and if it was sometimes difficult to convince him to experiment, he would always make time to study new ideas, even seemingly crazy ones, and accept periods of adjustment. For example, in 2009, he agreed to change his strings.

THE RACQUET AT THE CENTRE OF HIS ROUTINE

Rafa's racquet was central to his reassuring routines. Each time he came out on court and greeted the crowd, his Pure Aero was always in his hand. "As soon as I left the changing room, I'd simulate movements for hitting the ball," he explains. "It made me feel the match had already begun." Behind the scenes, his racquet fetish also played a part in his preparation. When he put on his ankle braces, he also put on the grips—size 2—that he would use throughout the match. "Generally, I played with racquets that I have already used in training. In my bag there were always six racquets that were numbered, so every time I knew which one I had in my hand. Mostly, I's begin playing with the one I'd used for the warm-up, which would have been strung just before the match." As for the strings, in 2021 Rafael Nadal switched from a 135 gauge to a 130 gauge (1.30 mm, equivalent to the diameter of the string), convinced that he could gain power. The tension —25 kg—and weight—317 g—on the other hand, never changed. "There were a few exceptions, for example if a match was being played at high-altitude, when I'd opt for a tension of 25.5 kg," he says.

OPPOSITE PAGE René Lacoste preparing his equipment in 1927 prior to facing the USA in the Davis Cup.

BELOW Almost 80 years later, Rafael Nadal follows the same routine.

FOLLOWING PAGES Rafael Nadal at the 2006 Roland–Garros final. He wins his second consecutive Roland–Garros title, defeating the world number one at the time, Roger Federer.

THE RPM REVOLUTION

Nadal had already won at Roland-Garros four times when he suffered his first defeat on the Paris clay court to Robin Söderling. It was an apocalyptic moment in the tennis world and shortly after this unprecedented defeat, the Spaniard, who had injured his knee, wanted to take advantage of his convalescence by making a few adjustments. Toni Nadal told Babolat that his nephew wanted to increase his ball length during play. The brand reacted swiftly by inviting Rafa to its Lyon premises in Gerland where they wanted to show him a brand new black string specially designed for his game. At the action stations in Lyon, the engineers had prepared Power-Point documents, statistical data and explanatory curves to show the champion how this new string would revolutionise his game. After their presentation, Nadal was in stitches when he answered them. "I really didn't understand your curves, but I'm sure they're all right!" This surreal scene demonstrates the level of confidence the champion had in the company manufacturing his equipment. The result was that when he tested this prototype on court, after just a few strokes, he loved it and then adopted it. In 2010, he took delivery of the new RPM Blast, an octagonal monofilament string that boosted not just spin but also power. He backed a winner, since during his first season with the RPM, Nadal achieved the Roland-Garros/Wimbledon double, before going on to win the US Open for the first time.

While Nadal's game evolved over the years and his range expanded, his racquet changed very little after 2004. Only micro-adjustments to weight and balance were made, since the fine-tuning of a frame is almost as precise as watchmaking. In 2012, and then again in 2017, two modifications were made and, for Rafa, that was always an event. "We were talking about 1 or 2 grams, which might seem ridiculous," says Jean-Christophe Verborg, "but at that level it multiplied the impact given the engagement of the players when they hit."

SPIN IS IN HIS DNA

Trajectories that curved to an extreme degree, a ball that kicked up on the bounce, a doomed opponent, Rafael Nadal's spin was always a sight to behold but it proved a living hell for the man on the other side of the net. It was the Spaniard's trademark, elevated to the level of an obsession. Since turning professional, Nadal had been able to whip the ball and make it oscillate with an extraordinary force estimated at 4,000 revolutions per minute, whereas Pete Sampras, in his day, could only reach 1,800 revolutions. His 'lasso' forehand—a word coined with Nadal in mind—was the best way to describe it. With this weapon, which he constantly perfected, and his characteristic finish with the racquet above his head, he was always able to push his rivals far back behind the baseline. Rafa's strength behind this shot lay in the rapid rotation of his wrist, a weapon that is extremely effective on clay, especially on the diagonal, when he succeeded in keeping his opponent on the backhand side.

RIGHT The entire range is dedicated to spin with the Pure Aero and RPM strings.

OPPOSITE PAGE Nadal plays a backhand at the end of the 2010 Australian Open.

FOLLOWING PAGES Rafael Nadal serves during his match against the Frenchman Gianni Mina at Roland-Garros in 2010.

AFFLELOU
PEUGEOT
BNP PARIBAS
PARIB

AFFLELOU
Orange sport
BNP PARIBAS
LONGINES
0:35
IBM

Rafael Nadal has an eye for detail and, with tennis, he sensed it in his entire being, playing every point as if his life depended on it. To give an example, during testing periods with Babolat, nothing slipped by the Spaniard, who could detect even the slightest irregularity. On one occasion, the team had brought ten prototypes to Manacor to work on his racquet handle and among these frames, one model was 2 millimetres longer. Not knowing this, Nadal picked the racquet up, hit a few balls and then immediately stopped. He then put the racquet next to his own to compare the sizes and immediately realised there was a difference. Similarly, when a special edition of his Pure Aero racquet was designed to celebrate his "decima," his ten victories at Roland–Garros, Babolat added fluorescent orange and red to the classic yellow of the frame, to match the Spanish flag. Very quickly, he pointed out that his visual cues had been altered. "During the first tests, he explained to us that he could see yellow at a point in his eye which was not normally there. But, true to form, he added, 'OK, I'll get used to it.'"

And so, for almost twenty–five years on the professional circuit, Rafael Nadal and Babolat learned and grew side by side. Together, they created strings, racquets and broke records, but, most of all, they were responsible for writing one of the finest pages in the history of world tennis, winning 92 ATP titles and a total of 24 Grand Slams.

A RACQUET WITH HIS NAME ON IT MODEL NO. 1

"I like powerful, bold colours and I loved this racquet because it looked like me," declares Rafael Nadal. "As a way of paying homage to his entire career, the French brand decided to create a stand–alone range, its first signature racquet. The Pure Aero Rafa was designed by him and he started using it in 2020. With this new frame, which features exclusive graphics, he won his 20th Grand Slam title at Roland–Garros.

RIGHT The Pure Aero Rafa comes close to the specifications of the racquet actually used by Rafael Nadal himself in terms of weight, balance, technology, rigidity, design and aesthetics.

OPPOSITE PAGE Rafael Nadal at Roland–Garros in 2014.

Babolat

THE RACQUET PLAYS A VITAL PART IN ANY PLAYER'S CAREER, IT'S AN EXTENSION OF OUR ARM AND WE EXPERIENCE EVERY SENSATION THROUGH IT. AT THE END OF THE DAY, IF WHAT YOU ARE FEELING IS NOT GOOD, IT IS VERY DIFFICULT TO ACHIEVE SUCCESS.

— Rafael Nadal

OPPOSITE PAGE Rafael Nadal holds the record for the most singles titles at Roland–Garros, having won 14 times between 2005 and 2022.

BELOW Rafael Nadal has twice won the Australian Open during the course of his career.

FOLLOWING PAGES Rafael Nadal against Ričardas Berankis at Wimbledon in 2022.

BAB O LAT

CHAMPIONS

IN THE 2000S, BABOLAT BECAME THE PREFERRED EQUIPMENT OF MANY TOUR CHAMPIONS

THE PURE AERO

OPTIMISED SPIN

THIS IS THE RACQUET FOR EXTREME SPIN. FEATURING THE WORLD'S FIRST AERODYNAMIC FRAME, IT PROMOTES A POWERFUL SPIN THAT BOOSTS OFFENSIVE PLAY AND PUSHES AN OPPONENT BACK BEHIND THE BASELINE. EVERY 2 MINUTES A BABOLAT PURE AERO RACQUET IS SOLD AROUND THE WORLD AND IT HAS BEEN ADOPTED BY ICONIC PLAYERS.

JO-WILFRIED TSONGA

The former French number one is a loyal fan of the Lyon-based brand, which he began using in 2017. Proud of being part of the Babolat family, he took French tennis to new heights. His record from 2004 to 2022 includes winning eighteen titles and an Olympic medal, as well as being a member of the victorious French team who won the Davis Cup, and reaching the final of the Australian Open. Now retired, the Frenchman is pursuing his 'second life' project, the development of the ALL IN group and its Lyon country club, Babolat's official partner for racquets, balls, string and luggage.

THE FIRST TIME I TRIED A BABOLAT RACQUET WAS WHEN ALL MY OLD ONES WERE BROKEN. I WAS PLAYING A TRAINING MATCH AND I WAS 5–2 DOWN IN THE FIRST SET ON CLAY. AT THAT TIME, MY RECORD ON THAT SURFACE WAS POOR SO I BORROWED A FRIEND'S RACQUET —AN AERO! I PLAYED 1.5 METRES LONGER AND I ENDED UP WINNING THE MATCH 7–5, 6–1. AFTER THAT, I DECIDED TO PLAY WITH THIS RACQUET AND I WAS ABLE TO PERFORM WELL ON CLAY THROUGHOUT MY CAREER, ESPECIALLY AT ROLAND-GARROS.

— Jo-Wilfried Tsonga

CAROLINE WOZNIACKI

In the search for power and control, the Danish player, a former World No. 1, chose the Pure Aero in 2013. She won the 2018 Australian Open and twice reached the final of the US Open. She was so attached to her racquet that in the second round of the 2014 US Open, her long hair literally became tied to the handle in the middle of a point. She tried to keep on playing "but it was impossible to untangle. When I attempted to hit the ball, I nearly pulled my hair out," she laughs.

PAULINE DÉROULÈDE

A leading player in wheelchair tennis, Pauline Déroulède has selected the Pure Aero to partner her during her greatest sporting moments: notably at the Paris 2024 Paralympics, where she was a member of the French team. Babolat will be beside her for the rest of her tennis journey.

BENOÎT PAIRE

A charistmatic player with a flamboyant style, Benoît Paire set the world alight with his Pure Aero racquet and Propulse Fury shoes. In partnership with Babolat since 2012, he acheived a world ranking of 18.

ADRIAN MANNARINO

A player unlike any other, Adrian Mannarino opts for very low tension, around 9–10 kg, compared to the majority of players on the circuit who tend to keep their racquets at between 22 and 25 kg.

CARLOS ALCARAZ

The Pure Aero helps to make the Spaniard's game even more spectacular. Thanks to his racquet, he is able to combine power and spin with better ball control. Something that's vital for the king of the drop shot!

THE PURE DRIVE

THE CLASSIC

THE BEST-SELLING RACQUET IN THE WORLD FOR MANY YEARS. ITS VERSATILITY IS ONE OF THE KEYS TO ITS SUCCESS AND IT IS EQUALLY SUITED TO BOTH PROFESSIONAL AND AMATEUR PLAYERS. THE PURE DRIVE'S DNA IS POWER AND EXPLOSIVENESS, WHATEVER THE SHOT, EVEN IF IT IS OFF-CENTRE, IN ADDITION TO EXCELLENT STABILITY AT THE POINT OF IMPACT.

FSI POWER TECHNOLOGY
CORTEX

ANDY RODDICK

The Pure Drive proved a real weapon of destruction for the American during his career, helping him rise to the top of the world rankings and win 32 titles, including the US Open in 2003.

KIM CLIJSTERS

The Belgian player fell in love with the Pure Drive when she was just 16. Since then she has never left it and still uses it several years after she retired.

AT HOME, I'VE HUNG THE RACQUETS I WON AT WIMBLEDON AND ROLAND-GARROS ON THE WALL, INCLUDING THE WHITE RACQUET THAT WAS SPECIALLY CUSTOMISED FOR WIMBLEDON. IT'S GREAT TO HAVE THESE TANGIBLE MEMORIES AND BE ABLE TO SHARE THEM WITH LOVED ONES. WHAT I LIKED WAS HOW THE PURE DRIVE HELPED ME TO BE AGGRESSIVE AND FEARLESS ON COURT.

— Garbiñe Muguruza

GARBIÑE MUGURUZA

With her Babolat racquet, she won ten WTA titles, including two Grand Slams at Roland–Garros and Wimbledon. Perfectly suited to her powerful game, her Pure Drive also enabled her to win the WTA Masters Finals at the end of the 2021 season.

KAROLÍNA PLÍŠKOVÁ

The Czech player has played with a Pure Drive since she was nine. "I've never wanted to change and I've never tried any other racquet as it's the best in the world." With the racquet, she has reached the number one spot in the world and two Grand Slam finals at Wimbledon and the US Open.

WHEN I SAW CARLOS MOYA WITH THIS RACQUET, I TOLD MY COACH THAT I WANTED TO TRY IT OUT. I THEN PLAYED IN A FUTURES TOURNAMENT IN MURCIA AND WON IT WITH THE PURE DRIVE. IT'S BEEN WITH ME EVER SINCE.

— Fabio Fognini

AS SOON AS I STARTED HITTING THE BALL WITH MY BABOLAT RACQUET, I KNEW IT WAS THE RIGHT ONE FOR ME. I LOVE BEING PART OF THE BABOLAT FAMILY AND I HAVE NEVER THOUGHT OF USING ANYTHING ELSE.

— Sofia Kenin

THE PURE STRIKE

ULTRA-PRECISION CONTROL

NOTHING COMPARES TO THE PLEASURE OF HITTING THE BALL EXACTLY WHERE YOU WANT IT TO GO. THE PRECISION CONTROL OF THE PURE STRIKE IS DESIGNED TO MEET THE NEEDS OF TENNIS PLAYERS WITH AGGRESSIVE AND POWERFUL GAMES. IT COMBINES DYNAMIC CONTROL AND REAL SENSATIONS FOR AN UNPRECEDENTED DEGREE OF RESPONSIVENESS, ALLOWING YOU TO DOMINATE THE COURT WITH EVERY SHOT.

DOMINIC THIEM

Winner of the US Open in 2020 and twice finalist at Roland–Garros, the Austrian has been playing with Babolat since the beginning of 2015.

BY THE TIME I DID MY FIRST PHOTOSHOOT WITH THE PURE STRIKE, IT HAD BECOME MUCH MORE COLOURFUL. ORIGINALLY, I HAD TO USE THE WHITE ONE FOR A FEW MONTHS, BUT THIS LATER VERSION PROVED SO POPULAR THAT BABOLAT KEPT IT. THE RACQUET HAD ALWAYS BEEN HERE, BY MY SIDE, ESPECIALLY DURING THE MOST IMPORTANT MOMENT IN MY CAREER WHEN I WON THE US OPEN. I SEE IT AGAIN BY MY FEET WHEN I'M ON THE GROUND.

— Dominic Thiem

ALIZÉ CORNET

The French player holds the record for the most Grand Slam appearances, a total of sixty-nine tournaments she played consecutively, all with a Babolat racquet. The brand has accompanied her since 2006.

CAMERON NORRIE

The British player chose the Pure Strike for its excellent balance between power and control. Loyal to Babolat since he was 12 years old, he has risen to 8th place in the world rankings and reached the semi-finals at Wimbledon.

NIELS VINK

With the Pure Strike, the Dutchman enjoyed the greatest triumph of all at the Paris 2024 Paralympics. By winning a gold medal for both singles and doubles in the Quad class, he has become even more of a wheelchair tennis legend.

THE PURE AERO RAFA

OPTIMISED SPIN

ITS SPECIFICATIONS REMAIN THE SAME AS THE PURE AERO BUT, WHAT SETS IT APART, IS A NEW EXCLUSIVE GRAPHIC REFLECTING THE PERSONALITY OF THE SPANISH CHAMPION.

RIGHT Rafael Nadal was involved in the concept of the Pure Aero Rafa, wanting the racquet to reflect the design of the Spanish flag.

PAGE 174 Rafael Nadal immediately after his victory against Novak Djokovic in 2020. It was his 13th Roland–Garros title.

Babolat
RAFA

I ALWAYS WORK TOWARDS A SPECIFIC GOAL: TO IMPROVE MYSELF NOT JUST AS A PLAYER BUT AS A PERSON AS WELL.

— Rafael Nadal

CORBAS
BABOLAT'S TECHNICAL HEADQUARTERS

Everything that contributes to making this family business so successful emanates from this place, a gigantic 24,000 square metre site where ideas are tossed around before taking shape. Corbas, to the south–east of Lyon, is the hub of Babolat's activities. It's here that discussions range from future innovation, Alcaraz's latest successes and even the racquet or tennis shoe of the future. Since 2012, this high–tech hangar has been home to the synthetic string factory, the research and development (R&D) laboratory, the Athletes' Service Workshop (S2A) for customising racquets and equipment and the logistics centre that supplies its products to sports shops and tennis clubs in 150 countries around the world.

ABOVE The production lines produce many kilometres of synthentic strings each week.

OPPOSITE PAGE Although the offices and production plant are historically based at Gerland, the synthetic string factory moved to Corbas on the outskirts of Lyon in 2017.

At Corbas, Babolat tests, try out and often discover what the firm is looking for. Their common goal gets elevated to the level of an obsession: to improve every day in order to move forward and set the standard. There are so many challenges, not to just meeting the demands of champions, but also those who just love tennis. Babolat's great strength has always been its ability to understand the needs of both club players and top-level athletes. A visit to Corbas begins in the research and development laboratory, where the high-volume products seen on shelves in stores around the globe are designed. It is in this top-level laboratory that ideas are collated, committed to paper then brought to life by the company's engineers. From stress tests to analysis benches, they take care of every last detail. They are to racquets and strings what a mechanic is on a race track to Formula 1 cars, in other words: an inseparable part of the team. In this scientific bubble, new products are designed and conceived using precision tools and custom-built machines. Prototypes of shoes are developed, wear and tear on balls is meticulously analysed, plus the time it takes for a racquet to become weakened and the number of strokes after which a string can break are calculated. The aim is to get as close as possible to what goes on in the game. What happens on court is then translated into curves, figures and statistics. It is in this way that Babolat can imagine the padel, badminton and tennis racquets of the future and hand them to a group of qualified testers. After mechanical tests have been carried out by machines, so-called "sensory" tests take place in the field. Babolat has its own network of players who undertake long-term tests. These are held in Lyon, Aix-en-Provence, Barcelona, Denver, Munich, Wimbledon and Tokyo for tennis, in Spain for padel and in China for badminton.

Because tennis is a sport based on personal sensation, devising a common language between the engineer and the player is not easy, as few people really know how to express what they feel. For this reason, it takes a year to qualify as a tester and once a player's feelings have been deciphered, a lot of follow-up to-ing and fro-ing is necessary. Products in development are tested, as well as standard equipment to check everything is still up-to-date, and sometimes products made by competitors too, so as to give a better understanding of the company's position in the market. Once a product is finalised, it is tested directly on end-use customers in key countries.

RIGHT The choice of string is made according to the desired effect. Strings are classified according to power, control, comfort and their lifespan.

OPPOSITE PAGE Synthetic strings now make up 82% of Babolat's production.

THE CUSTOMISATION SERVICE

A little further on, inside the warehouse, is an unassuming glass office housing contents worthy of Ali Baba's cave. There are boxes each containing six racquets, all packed, numbered, carefully prepared and ready for use. One of the boxes might discreetly bear the name Rafael Nadal, while another that of Karolína Plíšková or Carlos Alcaraz. For it is here, in the hands of Babolat's preparers, that the greatest victories have—and still do—take shape. It is the preparers who customise the racquets, some 2,000 are prepared during the year for the 200 professional players under contract with Babolat. Yes, it's true that great champions play with the same racquets as the average person, they are simply adapted and adjusted according to the individual player's needs and special features. Most importantly, sets consist of identical racquets so as not to distract a player during a match. Balance, weight and inertia are worked on as these are very fine adjustments customised to suit the individual player. Each player has six to twelve racquets in his or her bag, which are changed every three months. Specifications can change, when necessary, which is why Babolat's experts are there. With their unique and very detailed knowledge of the game, they have mastered all the parameters of the equipment they look after and are on the spot to detect any possible changes in the future. It's a full-time job of listening, sensitivity and trust. "We modify the shape of the handle, the balance and distribution of the weight and/or materials, to arrive at an ideal compromise between power and handling, techniques and objectives of the game," explains Sylvain Triquigneaux, head of the customisation service for professionals (S2A). "However, it is not always easy to decipher the player's feelings, what he or she is telling us, in order to help them by way of these adjustments to achieve their aim. It requires a lot of psychology and proximity." Professional players are also asked to help improve products, but the windows for this are much shorter. In general, everything happens during the winter preparation period, when the Babolat teams travel to training locations to work on the existing settings and achieve the best possible result.

THE SYNTHETIC STRING FACTORY

The driving force behind a racquet is its strings, which are also made at Corbas. The company makes miles of them, thanks to impressive production lines that operate 24 hours a day from Monday morning to midday on Saturday. The 'synthetic' is the combination of a touch of magic and a lot of chemistry. One of Babolat's special skills is the amalgamation of several types of polymer, beginning with polyester and polyamide. The core of the multifilament string is woven from several spools of polymer using threads finer than a single hair.

This is then cleaned in an alcohol bath, before other materials, in the form of granules, are added after melting.

The fibres are assembled by a process of extrusion, producing the string's core, with 24 hours being needed to produce 10 kilometres of string. The thread is then twisted, secured, glued and finally sheathed several times with polyamide and silicone, which makes the string smooth and the job of the stringer easier. A polyamide multifibre thread therefore follows a complex path before becoming a string with the desired texture, elasticity and resistance. The strings are then packed in individual 12-metre batches or 200 metre rolls for shops, professional stringers and tennis clubs. Whether monofilament or multifilament, synthetic represents 85% of Babolat's string output. It came into its own when natural gut became too expensive and styles of play began radically changing. The serve-volley approach gradually gave way to spin and, with it, the natural gut string to synthetic. Nowadays, players sometimes prefer hybrid strings, which combine the best of both worlds, half-gut, half-synthetic, with strings arranged according to their style of play.

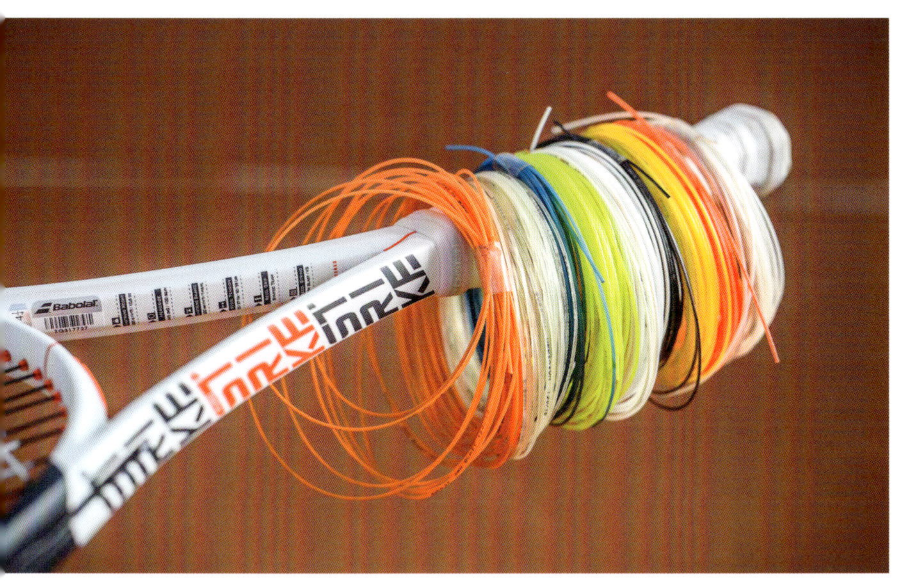

INTEGRATED EXTERNAL PARTNERSHIPS : THE EXPANSION OF THE COMPANY

Babolat has always looked for ways to progress and never hesitated to surround itself with outside companies in order to understand better how its equipment can be developed. To give an example, it draws on the know-how of the HumanFab® laboratory, an expert scientific and sports organisation that specialises in human engineering. The two companies are jointly pooling their expertise to improve Babolat's understanding of players, through scientific advances in the biomechanics of racquet sports. "Today, innovation in terms of equipment is based on empirical knowledge of players and in observing the game," explains Éric Babolat. "Our laboratory is the court and players all over the world, both in clubs and at the highest level. We are going to be able to deepen and refine this knowledge by approaching it in a scientific way, in order to come up with a very precisely adapted answer." This is how Babolat learnt there is a big difference in ball throwing between men and women and with this newly acquired knowledge they could adapt their equipment to the player, regardless of their age or level of play, to optimise performance and prevent certain injuries. When it comes to footwear, Babolat has also gone into partnership with the CTC—Centre Technique de la Chaussure (Footwear Technical Centre)—whose expertise lies in pumps and sports shoes. These studies provide in-depth knowledge of the particularities and dimensions of the foot on different continents, as well as the footwear habits of Babolat's different target audiences.

THE CONNECTED RACQUET ADVENTURE

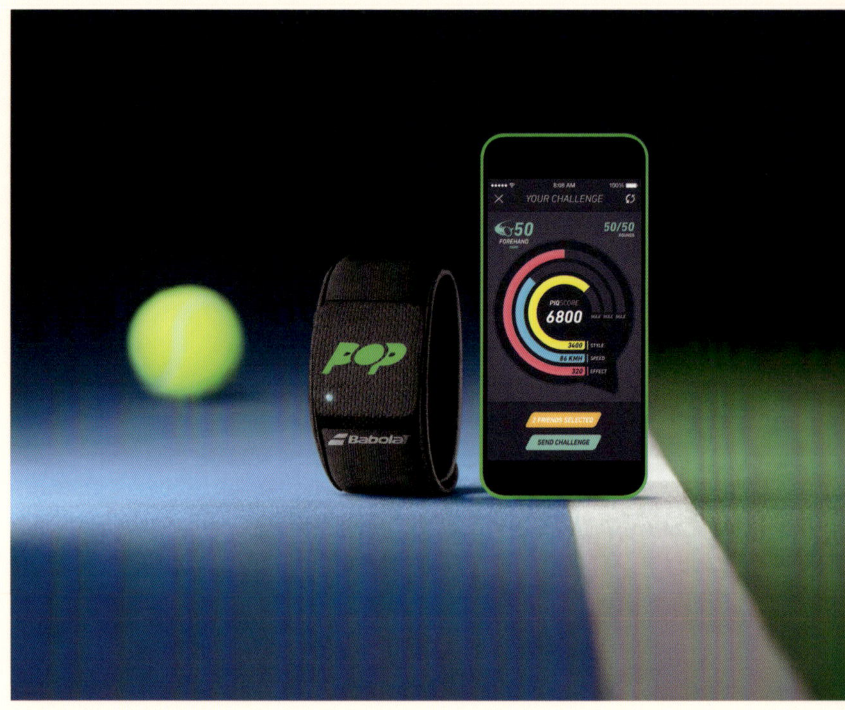

In 2012, Rafael Nadal became a 2.0 player and embarked on the adventure of the connected racquet, the first of its kind on the circuit. Thanks to sensors built into the handle, the Babolat Play was a new-generation racquet that enabled professional and amateur players to access and share new data, such as the speed of play and ball rotation in the ball-string impact zone.

Comparing his spin to that of Rafael Nadal, the idea is quite appealing. In the early 2010, at the start of the Big Data era, it is innovative and revolutionary. Tennis fans want to know everything,master everything and understand the game in its purest essence. Until then, Babolat engineers used a more empiric, human-based method. A panel of professional testers enables them to evaluate their innovations and develop new products. The protocol is tried and tested, but there are a few disadvantages. It takes time for a tester to qualify, a whole year for them to speak the same language as Babolat. After that, it is virtually impossible to be objective, as each evaluation incorporates cognitive biases. Those in Lyon did not give up and, at the end of several years of development, a very light electronic device had been developed. This consisted of a sensor, an accelerometer, a gyroscope and a battery, all built into a module that could be concealed in the handle of a racquet. It would not affect either the weight or overall balance of the frame and was universal, being aimed at club players and champions alike. All tennis fans could access new data, including the number of backhands or forehands played, the speed or rotation of the ball, in addition to being able to differentiate between spin, slice or flat shots, and the areas of impact on the racquet's strings. Data would be transmitted via Bluetooth, allowing players to share and analyse their performances.

Rafa was involved in the development of this new racquet and, in 2015, agreed to the module being added to his Pure Aero with the Babolat Play Aeropro Drive, despite it involving a slight change in his meticulous routine. It meant he now had to switch on his racquet before starting to play and then recharge it after each match! For Rafael Nadal it was an opportunity to analyse his game even more closely and to compare training sessions with matches. If, for example, he knew that he'd hit 70% forehands and 30% backhands, it was a good match. Toni Nadal made use of it, in particular, to optimise his training sessions. Rafa's uncle, always keen on advances in technology, was also interested in the area of impact where the ball came into contact with the strings when Rafael was serving.

Other players, such as Caroline Wozniacki and Mónica Puig, also experimented with a connected racquet over the years. It was deemed a 'nice thing to have' but remained a gadget that, over time, failed to become a 'must-have'. After eight years of experimentation, Babolat decided to withdraw its connected model from the market. However, it remains a source of pride for the family business, as it proved tennis could still be cool and trendy.

ABOVE Babolat is innovating once again, this time by giving amateur players the chance to compare their data with those of professional players.

OPPOSITE PAGE Launch of the Babolat Play at Roland-Garros in 2012 with Rafael Nadal and Éric Babolat.

THE 31ST RULE OF TENNIS

Until this time, electronic devices had been banned in tennis. With Babolat Play, the rules had to be changed and, to mark its centenary celebrations in Paris, the ITF passed the 31st rule of international tennis. Henceforth a tennis player could now compete while connected to an electronic device.

ALCARAZ

A NEW ADVENTURE

SINCE

2022

AFTER TWENTY STUNNING YEARS DEFINED BY THE TRIUMPHS OF RAFAEL NADAL, BABOLAT HAS SUCCEEDED IN BOUNCING BACK IN THE MOST DAZZLING FASHION BY ONCE AGAIN ALIGNING ITS DESTINY WITH THE VERY BEST. CARLOS ALCARAZ, IDOL OF A NEW GENERATION OF TENNIS FANS, HAS EMBODIED THE FAMILY BRAND'S VALUES FROM AN EARLY AGE.

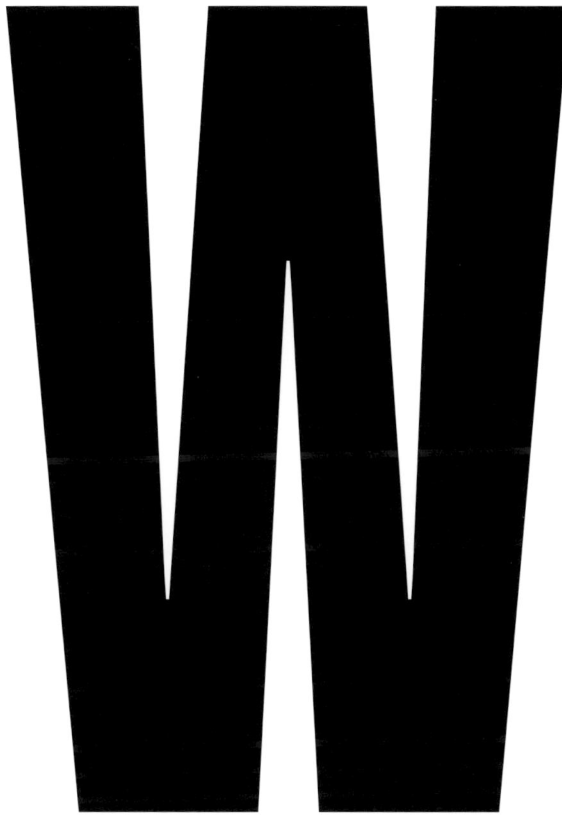

When Carlos Alcaraz Senior enrolled his son in the Club de Murcia in southern Spain, he gave him a priceless gift: a mini Babolat orange and neon fluo racquet, a Pure Aero Junior, which he cherished and carried with him in its little case everywhere he went. The young Carlos was just 4 years old at the time and, in 2007, the whole country only had eyes for a prodigy who was amassing titles. After his triumphs at Roland-Garros, 21-year-old Rafael Nadel had become a role model throughout Spain and, of course, the idol of little Carlos. In his apartment in El Palmar, where he lived with his parents, Carlos followed every one of Nadal's victories, every one of his matches, cheering him on in unison with the millions of Spaniards glued to their televisions. It was not long before, with the same racquet and the same frenzy, "Carlitos" was learning the basics of the sport, perfecting his skills and already making an impression. Like Rafa, he was gifted and precocious and by the time he was 10, he was getting noticed. Carlos won the "Babolat Cup" in Spain, a prestigious tournament bringing together the best prospects in his

OPENING At Wimbledon in 2023, Carlos Alcaraz overturns the four-time title holder Novak Djokovic and wins the tournament.

OPPOSITE PAGE Carlos Alcaraz is evolving with the Pure Aero model.

age group. The prize was a nice trophy to show off but, more importantly, it led to him signing his very first contract with Babolat. Very quickly, the family company was captivated by his game, recognising his great potential. Three years later, he was offered the chance to pursue his dream more seriously with the offer of an international contract. "Not only did he play well but he was already very happy on the court, just as he is today. He had something special and I wasn't the only one to think so," says Jean-Christophe Verborg, who was head of talent scouting at the time. At junior level, Carlos Alcaraz continued to shine, which was a godsend for Babolat, who had been looking to prepare for "life after Rafa."

I AM CONVINCED THAT CARLOS WILL GO VERY FAR, HE HAS ALL THE INGREDIENTS NEEDED TO BECOME AN EXCELLENT PLAYER AND THAT'S WHAT MATTERS.

— Rafael Nadal

LIFE AFTER RAFA

The company feared a generational slump and the prospect of a difficult period ahead when its great champion announced the end of his career. A successor, therefore, needed to be prepared years in advance with Babolat seeking to identify young talent as early as possible. "We didn't say categorically that he would be the one to take over, because a lot of things can happen and he could get injured," explains Jean-Christophe Verborg, "but it was crucial to sign players with such potential to succeed Rafa." With his energy, his smile and his raw talent, Carlos Alcaraz did not disappoint and he climbed the ladder remarkably quickly. Above all, he seamlessly negotiated the tricky transition into the professional world. His style of play was dazzling, as was his smile and, accompanied by his Pure Aero, the racquet that never left his side, he was a breath of fresh air on the tennis circuit. For his 18th birthday he received what was, potentially, the greatest gift of all, that of facing Rafael Nadal on the Manolo Santana Centre Court at the Madrid tournament. But a gift it wasn't to be and, in fact, he was soundly beaten (6–1, 6–2), but, nevertheless, it was a singular moment in his career. With his power and inspiration bordering on genius, Carlos caught the attention of the Spanish public and that of Rafael Nadal himself. "I am convinced that Carlos will go very far," Rafa said that day, "he has all the ingredients needed to become an excellent player and that's what matters." As a symbol of his meteoric rise, the following summer, when he turned 19, it was already time for his coronation. Carlos Alcaraz won the US Open in New York, his first ever Grand Slam title and the youngest ever world No. 1. He had just fulfilled his dream...and Babolat's.

ABOVE Tennis's new superstar, Carlos Alcaraz, has rapidly become the idol of the new generation.

FOLLOWING PAGES Carlos Alcaraz has been competing and winning matches with a Babolat racquet from a very young age.

2022

CARLOS ALCARAZ BECOMES THE YOUNGEST WORLD NO. 1 IN THE HISTORY OF TENNIS

Babolat

PARALLEL TRAJECTORIES

Another Spaniard, another talent with extraordinary values, another blazing racquet, the Pure Aero. This beguiling backdrop is, of course, reminiscent of Rafael Nadal's achievements, but that is where any comparisons with his illustrious predecessor end. Carlos Alcaraz refuses to define himself as the heir apparent: "There will not be another Rafa, I am Carlos," he likes to remind us. The two champions are, in fact, very different. Firstly, Carlos Alcaraz's game is so versatile that he is capable of attacking, getting to the net and producing exquisitely placed drop shots. There was the ultra-fighting spirit and the furrowed brow of the left-handed Rafa compared with the relaxed style and luminous smile of the right-handed Carlitos. "People have sometimes tried to pit them against each other but neither of them is disrespectful. Alcaraz was inspired by Nadal and feels extremely lucky to have been able to play alongside him," says Éric Babolat. His joie de vivre is infectious and his cool, fun side make him a role model for the new generation. Above all, he is very comfortable with his image. Less shy than Rafa was when he started out, he even enjoys fulfilling the many demands made on him. At the age of 20, Carlos Alcaraz has proved beyond doubt that he is not a flash in the pan. His first triumph in New York was quickly followed with an unforgettable victory at Wimbledon in 2023, against the defending champion, Novak Djokovic. This grass court thriller preceded another astounding display a year later on clay, Rafa's favourite surface. Triumphing at Roland-Garros sent out the powerful message that no surface could defeat him. Less than a month later, Carlos Alcaraz added a fourth major trophy to his impressive achievements at Wimbledon, confirming his undeniable appetite for breaking records.

RIGHT AND OPPOSITE PAGE Carlos Alcaraz is a versatile and spectacular player, capable of unleashing exquisite drop shots.

FOLLOWING PAGES Carlos Alcaraz at Wimbledon in 2023 and 2024.

LEFT AND BELOW Rafael Nadal and Carlos Alcaraz represent Spain at the Paris 2024 Olympic Games.

OPPOSITE PAGE The two men lose in the quarter-finals of the Olympics to Americans Austin Krajicek and Rajeev Ram. The match would be Rafael Nadal's last appearance at Roland-Garros.

PEOPLE HAVE SOMETIMES TRIED TO PIT THEM AGAINST EACH OTHER BUT NEITHER OF THEM IS DISRESPECTFUL. ALCARAZ WAS INSPIRED BY NADAL AND FEELS EXTREMELY LUCKY TO HAVE BEEN ABLE TO PLAY ALONGSIDE HIM.

— Éric Babolat

2024

OLYMPIC GAMES
ARE HELD IN PARIS

ABOVE In 2021, Alcaraz opted for the more accurate Pure Aero VS racquet, before switching to the Pure Aero 98 a year later.

OPPOSITE PAGE Alcaraz's racquet during the Mutua Madrid Open tournament in 2023.

PAGE 201 Crowned champion for the first time at Roland-Garros in 2024, Carlos Alcaraz becomes the youngest player to win a Grand Slam title on every surface.

HE STARTED TO WIN, AND WIN A LOT. CARLOS IS DEMANDING BUT NOW HE'S FOUND HIS WEAPON, THERE IS NO STRESS OR TENSION AROUND THE RACQUET. IN FACT, WE'VE RARELY HAD ANY.

— Jean-Christophe Verborg

A RACQUET MADE JUST FOR HIM

Carlos Alcaraz and Babolat are the "perfect match," the obvious choice so sought after by the family firm. With its new prodigy, the company has proved that its fortunes are not simply reliant on Rafael Nadal. Above all, it is the result of a gamble 10 years ago and the outcome of intense work by their scouting teams. "The cynics said 'Babolat IS Nadal and when Nadal goes, that will be it.' But then, along comes a super-charismatic champion who wins everything. It just proves that Babolat has known how to spot talent and personality since the days of René Lacoste and Suzanne Lenglen," says Éric Babolat proudly. With enthusiasm, motivation and strong family values, Carlos Alcaraz perfectly reflects the ethos of the Babolat group. He is also the injection of new blood that tennis needed. After years of domination by the Big 3 (Nadal, Federer and Djokovic), Carlitos is spearheading a new generation that is taking over. An icon of his sport, he is now the one who inspires and creates vocations among the youngest players. "He's a sporting superhero and people want to imitate his game, his look and his behaviour." adds the President. But, above all, they want to have the same racquet! The famous Pure Aero, the same as Rafa's, with its frame dedicated to spin and which has undergone a few changes over the years. In 2021, Carlos decided on the Pure Aero VS, a racquet with extra precision. "I wanted to have a bit more control," he explains. "I saw this racquet had an extra string and I wanted to try it out. I really like it because the ball leaves the strings so fast and it also allows me to increase in confidence and control," adds the young champion. This Babolat Pure Aero VS has a smaller head measuring 632 cm^2 (compared to the Pure Aero's 645 cm^2) and its frame, which has a slightly square profile, is also slimmer, while still retaining a dynamic racquet style. Shortly after, in 2022, Carlos finally switched to the Babolat Pure Aero 98, which was an advanced version of the Pure Aero VS and equipped with RPM Blast strings. For the young Spaniard, this racquet change was smooth and done in close collaboration with Babolat. It all started in 2020, when Carlos's agent, Albert Molina, called their teams with a very specific request. Because he had gained muscle mass, Carlos was finding his old racquet too powerful. His need was taken on board but, coming in the middle of the COVID-19 epidemic, it was difficult to respond quickly as teams could not travel or carry out live tests. Regardless, Babolat bent over backwards to come up with a solution. Two different models of racquets were sent to him, including the one Carlos uses today, and the result has exceeded expectations. "He started to win, and win a lot. Carlos is demanding but now he's found his weapon, there is no stress or tension around the racquet. In fact, we've rarely had any," explains Jean-Christophe Verborg. "It's more than just a tennis racquet," continues Carlos, now a fully-fledged member of the Babolat family. "There are people at Babolat who I consider to be part of my team and they listen carefully to my needs and feedback." Communication between Carlos and Babolat is seamless, marked with simplicity, and, above all, made easier by those around him, in particular his family and his coach, Juan-Carlos Ferrero. "This respect for the way things are done gives us confidence in the future as Carlos is not a meteorite," affirms Éric Babolat. Rather than a meteorite, Carlos Alcaraz is a star that will shine for Babolat until at least 2030. As in Rafa's time, he has been offered a long-term contract to ensure his loyalty. "I had no reason to go in search of another brand," says a delighted Carolos, who, with Babolat, continues the great history of tennis, a story that begin in 1875.

I SAW THIS
RACQUET HAD
AN EXTRA STRING AND
I WANTED TO TRY IT OUT.
I REALLY LIKE IT BECAUSE
THE BALL LEAVES THE STRINGS
SO FAST AND IT ALSO
ALLOWS ME TO INCREASE
IN CONFIDENCE
AND CONTROL.

— Carlos Alcaraz

NIKE
SIMPLE MESSIEURS

2024

CARLOS ALCARAZ
WINS ROLAND–GARROS

THE PRESENT AND THE FUTURE

TO ENSURE IT CAN CONTINUE TO SUCCESSFULLY IDENTIFY THE NEW NADAL OR TOMORROW'S CARLITOS, BABOLAT HAS ALWAYS INVESTED IN YOUTH AND POTENTIAL TALENT OF THE FUTURE. LOYALTY AND A LONG-TERM APPROACH ARE THE CARDINAL VIRTUES OF THIS INTENSIVE DETECTIVE WORK. THE COMPANY TAKES AN INTEREST IN YOUNG PLAYERS VERY EARLY ON, BEFORE THEIR BODIES HAVE REACHED MATURITY AND—IF THEY ARE BOYS—BEFORE THEIR VOICES HAVE BROKEN, THE VERY TIME WHEN IT IS MOST DIFFICULT TO GET A CLEAR PICTURE. HOWEVER, BABOLAT REALISES IT IS NECESSARY TO TRY, TO DARE PLACE A BOLD BET, WHILE ALL THE TIME ADHERING TO THE COMPANY'S CORE VALUES OF LOYALTY AND RESPECT.

ABOVE When you watch him playing with his Pure Aero, there's always something going on. Holger Rune is a raw talent and a player of character. This great hope of world tennis put his faith in Babolat at the age of 16 on the advice of his coach Patrick Mouratoglou.

LEFT Juncheng Shang is at the forefront of a new generation of Chinese players. In 2024, he became the first Chinese teenager to break into the ATP top 100.

OPPOSITE PAGE In possession of a devastating serve and a well-honed physique, Arthur Fils, born in 2004, is the rising star of French tennis. His aggressive style of play is highlighted by his racquet, the Pure Aero 98, and its RPM Blast strings. Using the same weapons as Carlos Alcaraz and Holger Rune, he can vary the amount of spin he uses while maintaining maximum control.

DISCOVERING NEW TALENTS

Initially relationships are usually established when youngsters are around 10–12 years of age. During the course of lengthy discussions with parents and coaches, Babolat assesses the potential and abilities of each. Identifying this as early as possible is crucial as few players switch equipment manufacturers during their careers. "The racquet is their hand and they prefer to progress using equipment they have already mastered," says Éric Babolat. But above and beyond recruitment, it is also vital to understand how to support a young talent. Physical development, injuries, adapting to the environment and mental strength are all unknown factors in the equation for identifying a champion of the future. "We do our best to guide young athletes as much as possible but to respect them, as it's not in anyone's interest for them to burn out or get injured," explains Jean-Christophe Verborg, from the competition department. The family aspect of the company is also something that can be reassuring, so Éric Babolat focuses on co-signing all the young international players' contracts.

RIGHT Leylah Fernandez, born in 2002, has always held a Babolat racquet in her hand. The Pure Aero enabled her to reach the US Open Final in 2021 and win several titles on the WTA Tour.

OPPOSITE PAGE TOP Sāra Bejlek during the first round of the 2024 Australian Open.

OPPOSITE PAGE BELOW Laura Samson reached the French Open junior final at Roland-Garros in 2024.

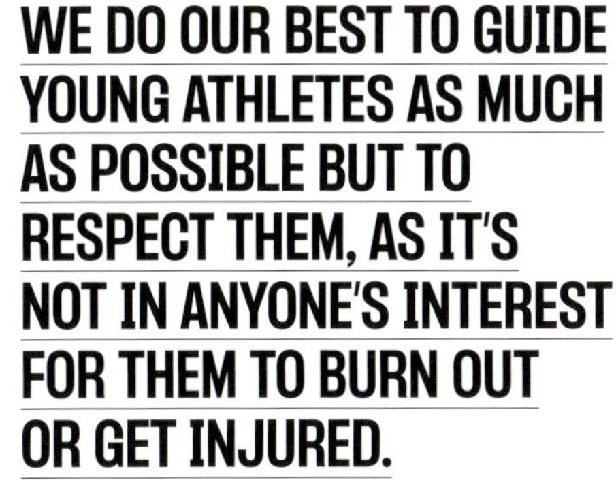

WE DO OUR BEST TO GUIDE YOUNG ATHLETES AS MUCH AS POSSIBLE BUT TO RESPECT THEM, AS IT'S NOT IN ANYONE'S INTEREST FOR THEM TO BURN OUT OR GET INJURED.

— Jean-Christophe Verborg

RBEL
POWER

BADMINTON, PADEL AND PICKLEBALL

COMPETING COUSINS

Over the past 150 years, Babolat has invested a great deal of enthusiasm and energy into the development of other racquet sports, such as badminton and the newest members of the family, padel and pickleball. They are fun, accessible sports that have encouraged the brand to diversify and broaden its horizons. From its long-standing expertise in making strings from natural gut, to developing an entire kit, Babolat has applied the same principles of universality and expertise to badminton, padel and pickleball, winning over champions and amateur players alike.

BADMINTON, BETWEEN LIGHTNESS AND INTENSITY

Badminton is a sport that calls for lightness, jumping and twirling. It is also about watching the progress of an object floating through the air as it is struck by blows and steered by strokes. Behind these stop-start movements are players seemingly mounted on springs, who compete in strategy and technique for this aesthetically choreographed game of chess. More physically demanding than you might think, badminton can often surprise you by its intensity, while at the same time proving to be just as much fun when you fancy trying to play. It was therefore unthinkable for Babolat to miss out on this phenomenon and, initially, it was an opportunity for the Lyon-based brand to diversify and capitalise on its core business—its expertise in manufacturing strings. From the outset the brand did what it knew best, making VS quality strings—as they already made for tennis—but adapting them to the needs of badminton. Thus, the strings became thinner, less elastic and shorter, while the research and development principles remained exactly the same. Success was immediate and Babolat won numerous international tournaments with their VS string. Later, things turned serious when the firm from Lyon decided to expand its production, offering a complete range of bags, shuttlecocks, grips, shoes, outfits and, of course, racquets. It was 1995 and badminton, already very popular in Asia, had just recaptured the hearts of Europeans. It was the rediscovery of an old sport that had been played at the beginning of the 20th century in France, Germany, England and Scandinavia, and the craze for it was total. And so, a century after tennis racquets, Babolat launched its very first range of badminton racquets, while simultaneously creating a separate division entirely dedicated to the sport. A new audience was targeted since badminton, an indoor sport and one that was easily accessible, was also inexpensive (an entry level racquet cost about 20 euros). Since then, a wide range of racquets, designed to suit all levels of play and all types of players, has been available. As with tennis, the brand strives to meet the needs of every player. With badminton, the tradition of innovation continues and frames include the latest advances in the improvement of power, control and comfort. For example, this can be seen in the "Metric Flex" technology, which makes it possible to vary the flexibility of the racquet according to the power of the stroke. The reason for this is that, unlike tennis, in badminton the string no longer acts as a motor but as a shaft—or rod—allowing the player to generate speed. Thanks to Babolat's reputation and the quality of its products, it has quickly gained momentum in the badminton world, even managing to attract top-class players.

Badminton has been an Olympic sport since 1992 but by the 2000s it was very common in schools and even became one of the most popular sports in secondary and high schools. Aware of this trend, Babolat continued to innovate by creating teaching kits—just as Major Wingfield had done for tennis in 1874—to enable young people to learn to play the sport under the best conditions. PE teachers were given around twenty racquets, shuttlecocks and a small net, plus a detailed guide on the best way to teach the sport.

THE WORLD'S NUMBER 2 AMBASSADOR

When you come from Asia and are a professional badminton player, putting your trust in a French equipment manufacturer is quite unusual. Hongyan Pi, however, decided to take the risk. She had been dropped from the Chinese national team when she was 20 as she was deemed too small and her play insufficiently attacking. Despite being just 1.64 metres tall, she refused to give up and decided instead to try her luck in Europe, first in Denmark, where Babolat spotted her playing in a tournament. "I didn't speak French and, at the time, I didn't know the brand," she recalls. "I had to get used to this new racquet but, pretty quickly, the range was perfected and I really enjoyed playing with the different models." In both badminton and tennis, the approach is the same: to rely on inspiring champions for its development. As with many of the athletes Babolat has supported, Hongyan has seen the brand's expansion into the world of badminton and has not hesitated to offer invaluable advice on everything from racquets to clothing. "To begin with, we were playing in shorts and t-shirts that didn't fit very well, but fortunately they listened to what I told them," she says with a smile. At the end of 2003, Hongyan moved to France, became a French citizen and joined the national team. More than simply having the satisfaction of getting her own back, it proved a unique opportunity for her. She reached No. 2 in the world rankings, won numerous titles and a bronze medal at the world championships. She also represented France at three Olympic Games—in Athens, Beijing and London—always with her Babolat racquet, which she never stopped using. As well as her attachment to the brand that has supported her financially for all these years, she likes how comfortable the racquets are to play with and the company's continual desire to innovate. During her career, Hongyan has also been involved in developing shoes designed especially for badminton. Drawing on her own experiences and sensations on court, she has advised Michelin's designers so that the soles of the shoes are as close as possible to the needs of the badminton players. "I explained to them how we move around the court and where we needed more support in a shoe," adds Hongyan, who still maintains a strong link with Babolat by continuing to work with them as a consultant.

She is also helping this family firm tackle the major challenge of breaking further into the Asian market, especially in China, where it is still difficult to establish a foothold. "People know our brand and they like it but there is still a lot of competition. We need to persuade people to change their habits."

The French brand has opened offices in Shanghai to monitor its business there as closely as it can and with the determined ambition of seeing the "French touch" attract the continent a little more.

OPPOSITE PAGE Badminton player Chloe Birch at the 2019 European Games where she wins gold in the women's doubles with her teammate Lauren Smith.

RIGHT Hongyan Pi with her Shadow Tour shoes and her X-Feel racquet during the 2012 Summer Olympics in London.

SHOES DESIGNED SPECIFICALLY FOR BADMINTON

Babolat also offers its expertise and has entered into partnerships to further badminton's development. In 2009, again in association with Michelin, a shoe was designed especially to meet the specific needs of the sport. Badminton is played indoors with the emphasis on high leaps rather than lateral movement. The soles of the shoes therefore need to be lighter to provide foot stability and their style adapted to the three dimensions. Two main ranges are currently available: Shadow Tour and Shadow Spirit, which meet all the necessary requirements for comfort, support and grip.

ABOVE Joachim Persson in the first round of the Yonex All England Badminton Open Championship in 2011.

RIGHT Aamir Ghaffar during the English Open in 2005.

OPPOSITE PAGE Ronan Labar and Lucas Corvée at the 2024 French Badminton Championships.

PADEL, THE UP-AND-COMING SPORT

When you play it for the first time, chances are you'll be immediately hooked, as padel is a sport that makes you smile. In the space of a couple of hours, you'll have fun, make progress and then, with the game barely over, you'll want to play it all over again. Surrounded by glass walls that the ball can be bounced off and therefore allowing a point to last indefinitely, it is the fun sport *par excellence* and the fastest growing in the world. Plus, it has a huge following— around 13 million players in 110 different countries. It is already estimated that, within the next decade or so, there will be as many padel players as there are tennis players, a total of around 90 million! With a figure such as this, it really must be love at first sight. But beyond becoming a widespread addiction, padel is also a way of life. The game encourages social interaction and appeals to all backgrounds and generations. "Clubs have become real meeting places for all. In the morning, the pros train, then it's the turn of those who have retired. Between noon and two in the afternoon, company executives take a break there and, in the evening, friends meet, first to have a good time on court, then followed by a move to the bar," says Éric Babolat, whose company was a frontrunner in the padel story, back in 2003. Initally, it was the Babolat teams based in Spain who were alerted to this new craze, which was all the rage on the other side of the Pyrenees. In the homeland of Rafael Nadal, padel had been booming since the early 2000s, being the second most popular "team" sport after football. Spain is the world centre of padel, with 2,800 clubs, which, in terms of market share, is twice as many as tennis. Straight away, the Lyon-based company launched its first range of racquets, exclusively for the Spanish market. The reason for this was simple: Babolat wanted to learn and understand more about the nature of this new sport. The feedback was very positive so, fifteen years later, when padel really took off in France, the company had already built up a certain level of expertise so everything could be accelerated. A padel division was created in Madrid with a dedicated team in place and, last but by no means least, Babolat padel equipment were marketed throughout Europe. Over the past four years, sales of racquets have broken records, rising from 2 million to 4.5 million worldwide, with the brand using the same formula that made it successful in tennis, which, it goes without saying, getting inspiring champions involved.

PADEL, WHAT IS IT?

Similar to tennis, padel (the name comes from the English "paddle"), is played on a synthetic turf doubles court measuring 20 x 10 m, with a net across the centre and surrounded by glass walls that can be used when playing the game. The sport was born in Mexico, developing more precisely in Acapulco where, in 1969, an entrepreneur named Enrique Corcuera adapted a piece of land, originally a pelota court, by building walls on the sides and back to protect it from encroaching vegetation. He quickly realised that players were allowing the ball to bounce off the opposite wall of the court and, in so doing, creating a new surface that could be used during play. There were no strings this time in the racquet, it was perforated with different-sized holes to reduce its weight and allow the ball to move more easily through the air. The maximum dimensions of the racquet are 45.5 cm long and 26 cm wide. Originally made of wood, these days racquets are made of fibreglass or carbon fibre.

OPPOSITE PAGE Babolat begins the padel adventure in 2003.

PADEL CLUBS HAVE BECOME REAL MEETING PLACES FOR ALL. IN THE MORNING, THE PROS TRAIN, THEN IT'S THE TURN OF THOSE WHO HAVE RETIRED. BETWEEN NOON AND TWO IN THE AFTERNOON, COMPANY EXECUTIVES TAKE A BREAK THERE AND, IN THE EVENING, FRIENDS MEET, FIRST TO HAVE A GOOD TIME ON COURT, THEN FOLLOWED BY A MOVE TO THE BAR.

— Éric Babolat

JUAN LEBRÓN — BABOLAT IN STEP WITH "THE WOLF"

"With Babolat, I wanted to take padel to the four corners of the world," such was the ambition of Juan Lebrón, one of the greatest players of his generation. In 2019, he made history by becoming the first Spaniard to be ranked number one in the world and, in a sport that had long been dominated by the Argentinians, it was an impressive achievement. "It was one of the most important moments of my life and living it with the Babolat family, who always believed in me, made it even more special," he says. "It is something I will never forget."

Lebrón and Babolat were an obvious match. Babolat's scouts had spotted the player in 2016 during the World Padel Tour, a global padel circuit at that time. He stood out by breaking the rules with his ultra-attacking game, far from what was expected at that time. "We imagined a new padel racquet in his hands and believed he could epitomise the evolution of the game in the coming years," explains Frédéric Bertucat Martinez, Babolat's International Padel Development Director. It was a premonitory vision since, in the space of five years, Juan Lebrón took his sport into a new dimension, one that focused on speed and spectacular style. "He was totally committed to this sport and dreamed of being the LeBrón James of padel," says Jean-Christophe Verborg. Gifted with a strong, sometimes abrasive, personality, he was nicknamed "El Lobo" (the wolf, in Spanish) and in recognition of this, whenever he hits a winning smash, tradition demands the crowd imitates the howl of his *alter ego* in the animal kingdom. Just as Rafael Nadal has his bull logo, Juan Lebrón has his own signature racquet. The "Juan Lebrón Technical Viper" is a carbon fibre racquet that offers extreme power and maximum spin, staying true to the player's DNA and fighting spirit.

ABOVE Juan Lebrón and Alejandro Galán before their match in the final of the Premier Padel at Madrid in 2022.

OPPOSITE PAGE Juan Lebrón with his famous racquet bearing the wolf logo.

LAMBORGHINI X BABOLAT

It was this collaboration of two iconic brands that took padel into another dimension. In 2024, Babolat called upon Automobili Lamborghini, the absolute benchmark in carbon manufacturing, to produce a very limited range of a legendary racquet: the BL001. Directly inspired by the hypercar chassis, this collector's item combined two technological and industrial visions in the creation of an exceptional product. The model, produced in a limited edition of just fifty, combined the carbon fibre characteristic of Lamborghini sports cars with Babolat's experience in make padel equipment. Six months of research were necessary to develop the racquet which combined power and luxury with perfect control and absolute comfort. Two other racquets inspired by this model would be developed at the BABOLAT PADEL STUDIO, based in Barcelona, designed to appeal to a wider audience.

REVOLUTIONARY SHOES

In 2019, Babolat was the first brand to develop shoes purely for padel, in collaboration with its longstanding partner, Michelin. The Jet Premura proved a great hit with the public and was even voted "Shoe of the Year" in Spain in 2019 and 2020. Rapidly adopted by Juan Lebrón, the design of the shoes facilitated changes of direction and movement, specific to padel, from front to back. With the choice of a unique ankle support, more weight and a sole adapted to withstand 3D jumps, Babolat had channelled all its expertise into the creation of the shoe.

IT WAS ONE OF THE MOST IMPORTANT MOMENTS OF MY LIFE AND LIVING IT WITH THE BABOLAT FAMILY, WHO ALWAYS BELIEVED IN ME, MADE IT EVEN MORE SPECIAL. IT IS SOMETHING I WILL NEVER FORGET.

— Juan Lebrón

PICKLEBALL, A NEW SPORT FOR THE FUTURE?

BELOW The Babolat MNSTR+ is the perfect racquet for competitive players looking for powerful performance.

OPPOSITE PAGE Babolat embarks on its pickleball (a mix of tennis, badminton and table tennis) adventure with RBEL and RNGD racquets. In 2021, the brand unveils two new ranges, launching MNSTR and XPLR.

An intense exchange of pickleball will keep those watching on the edge of their seats and a spectator's attention will be immediately drawn to the unique sound of the plastic ball. Using a combination of finesse, speed and precision, players compete with strategy and skill to win. There was no way that Babolat could miss out on this emerging new phenomenon.

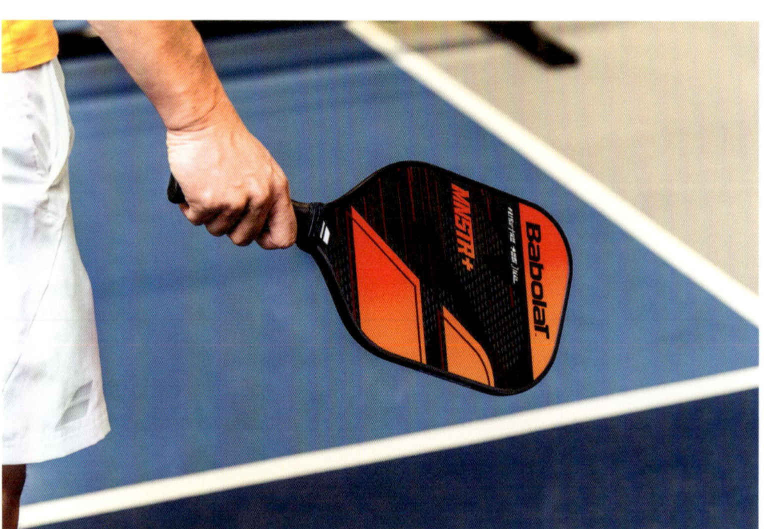

Pickleball exploded as a sport in the US in 2004 and, over the course of the next five years, the number of players increased from 2.5 to 4.2 million, while club memberships by more than 1000%. Fronted by two high-profile ambassadors named Steffi Graf and André Agassi, it is the latest addition to the family of racquet sports. A mix of tennis, badminton and table tennis, it is played with a carbon fibre racquet on a small court. As with padel, the game is great fun and has an appeal that stretches beyond the realms of tennis. Children, young adults and senior citizens all love pickleball and, the good news is, you don't need technique to enjoy playing it. It's a bit like bowling or playing with beach racquets. As with padel, pickleball brings people together, creating social bonds, as there is something to appeal to all tastes and levels. It is a sport for everyone that Babolat really enjoys and the brand is taking a close interest in it, with the aim of becoming a major player in its development. In 2020, the company set out on their 'great pickleball adventure' launching equipment designed in a modern, eye-catching style. Central to the BPKL (standing for 'Be Pickle'), two ranges of racquets were unveiled—the RBEL and RNGD—followed, in 2021 by the MNSTR and XPLR ranges. Babolat's ambition is clear: to use their 150 years of know-how and expertise to support the development of pickle as closely as they can. The pickleball craze promises to become a major success in the years to come. What remains to be resolved is the sensitive issue of pickle and tennis existing side by side. While some see the emergence of this new sport posing a threat to the future of tennis, Babolat looks on it as an additional asset and an opportunity to diversify.

JET FEEL: THE SHOE OF THE FUTURE

What if the future was synonymous with pleasure? To this end, Babolat has continued to innovate again and again, this time by designing the lightest shoe in the world. Weighing just 310g, the Jet Feel promises to give a player the sensation of flying, it will be like slipping a glove on their foot. Once again in collaboration with Michelin designing the soles and with a Matryx textile upper, their aim has been to revolutionise movement on the court by offering every player the perfect balance between performance and agility.

Babolat
MNSTR

Since 1875, the company's spirit of innovation and openness, as well as being resolutely entrepreneurial with its sights fixed on the future and emerging new trends, has enabled it to capitalise on its history and experience to design and produce the best equipment for lovers of tennis, badminton and padel. It all began with mastering how to process raw animal intestines to produce the first tennis racquet strings made of natural gut. Immediately adopted in the 1920s by players and history's first champions—René Lacoste, Jean Borotra, Henri Cochet and Toto Brugnon, who were known as the French Tennis Musketeers, as well as 'the divine' Suzanne Lenglen. These sporting heroes inspired the whole world with their exploits, both in the Davis Cup and in the Grand Slam tournaments at Wimbledon, New York, Roland-Garros and in Australia. As sport and leisure developed into social activities, the number of tennis and badminton players grew not just in Europe, but from the Atlantic to the Urals, across the Commonwealth and the United States, in Argentina, in Japan, around the Mediterranean and elsewhere. The emergence after the Second World War of newly developed synthetic materials led to strings being invented that had more resistance and were cheaper, as well as grips that absorbed perspiration more efficiently than leather. In addition, the process of stringing racquets shifted away from being done solely by hand to using electric machines that produced higher tensions in a more precise and even way. Learning to play sport for recreation and in competition became more democratic and the fun aspect of "games" promoted physical and psychological good health. In 1969, when Enrique Corcuera invented padel in Mexico, an "easy" version of tennis, he paved the way for a game that was rapidly adopted by Argentina and Spain and would win over Europe and the rest of the world.

The presence of its brand at different sports grounds, private clubs and public courts, as well as professional racquet preparers and stringers, plus the best competitors in more than 150 countries around the world, means Babolat can easily learn and anticipate what lovers of tennis, badminton and padel need. High-level involvement with competitors, whether able-bodied or disabled, from an early age, is the laboratory for the most advanced practical experience. The passion of these athletes, their entourage and the professionals who support them, including our teams and their representatives, fuels their dreams and motivates them to surpass themselves in all areas of their performance. How proud we are to win Grand Slams or gold medals and to make sporting and world history with our champions and their sporting "families," some of whom we've been a part of for several generations!

Arthur Ashe, the American champion who made history around the world with his sporting talent and his political commitment—coupled with the charismatic French champion Yannick Noah, as well as Björn Borg, Stan Smith, Martina Navratilova, Jan Kodeš, Ilie Nastase, Guillermo Vilas, Mats Wilander, Stefan Edberg, Pete Sampras, Boris Becker, Martina Hingis, Arantxa Sánchez and her brothers Emilio and Javier, Camilla Martin with her strings, grips and accessories, and then Kim Clijsters, Andy Roddick, Fernando Gonzales, Peter Gade Rasmussen, Mónica Puig, Francesca Schiavone, Carlos Moya, Àlex Corretja, Jo-Wilfried Tsonga, Hongyan Pi, Rafael Nadal, Stéphane Houdet, Caroline Wozniacki, Garbiñe Muguruza, Juan Lebrón, Félix Auger-Aliassime, Carlos Alcaraz, Niels Vink, Leo Borg, Arthur Fils, Pauline Déroulède, among many others in all parts of the world, for whom we have made racquets, strings and, increasingly, shoes...Talented, inspiring and charming champions whose ambitions, joys and sorrows we have shared during the preparation and participation in competitions and often in their post-sporting careers.

The company's extended international family, both on court and in the preparation of equipment, along with devotees of our sports, both top athletes and amateurs alike, share the love of these sports and the personal and collective development they bring.

These deep global roots are inextricably linked with the wings of progress and that of surpassing oneself to go ever further!

— Éric Babolat

ACKNOWLEDGMENTS

On behalf of all tennis, badminton, padel and pickleball enthusiasts, I would like to thank the company entrepreneurs who preceded me, and especially those in my family, for making Babolat their favourite brand.

When Rafael Nadal is asked about the reasons for his success, he simply answers: "I love what I do, and every day I strive to improve."

I share this vision and strive to apply it. I feel that this state of mind is that of the Babolat family; the Babolat family extended to all those who have been close to us, collaborators, and partners for 150 years.

Those who are passionate about our sports live it every day in their clubs and academies around the world, with their teams and teaching pros. I would like to thank in particular the Rafa Nadal academies and foundation, Carlos Alcaraz's Murcia Escuela de Tenis, Jo-Wilfried Tsonga's Allin, the Juan Carlos Ferrero Academy and the Court 16 clubs, among the many Babolat partner clubs around the world.

I'd also like to thank all the racquet tuners and stringers around the world who help us fine-tune the equipment we use.

I'd also like to thank our partners, the globally inspiring brands Wimbledon, Michelin and Club Med.

Together, we nurture the love of the game in the lives and minds of enthusiasts: thank you!

— Éric Babolat

CREDITS

© AFP / p. 74 top and bottom: Gabriel Duval. © Alamy Banque d'Images / p. 8: Nicolas Gouhier/ABACAPRESS.COM; p. 33 middle: PA Images; p. 42: GL Archive; p. 63: Trinity Mirror/Mirrorpix; p. 66 top: Keystone Press; p. 82: Smith Archive; p. 210: Sport In Pictures. © Archives Babolat / p. 4–5: Matthieu Latry; p. 6–7: Christian Chaize; p. 16, 17, 18 left, 19, 20–21, 24, 28, 29, 37 bottom, 44, 45 top, 46, 47; p. 48, 50 top: Stéphane Rambaud; p. 50 bottom; p. 51, 52 and 53: Stéphane Rambaud; p. 54, 55, 56–57, 60, 62, 66 bottom, 69, 70 bottom, 78, 79, 83, 84, 85, 86, 94, 95, 96, 99, 106, 110–111, 114, 115, 116, 121 top, 126, 128, 134, 148–149, 158–159, 166–167; p. 173: Studio Les Lumineurs; p. 176, 178 top, 178 bottom, 179, 180, 181: Stéphane Rambaud; p. 182, 183, 204 bottom, 207 bottom, 208; p. 213 : Yohan Nonotte/Badmintonphoto; p. 215; 217 right: Lemon Studio; p. 218, 219, 220. © BNF / p. 23, 26, 30–31, 32 left, 34, 37 top, 38–39, 117 bottom. © Bridgeman Images / p. 13. © CCO / p. 14, 18 right. © Antoine Couvercelle / p. 100–101, 107, 108–109, 112–113, 113, 117 top, 119, 120, 131, 132–133, 135, 138 top, 138 bottom, 139, 140, 143, 150–151, 152, 154, 161, 162–163, 164, 165 bottom, 169, 170, 172, 174, 185, 186, 189, 191, 194, 195, 199, 201, 202–203, 205, 206. © Chryslène Caillaud/Gianni Ciacia/Sportvision / p. 43, 76, 77, 81, 87 left, 87 right, 88, 89 left, 89 right, 91, 97 left, 97 right, 104, 124, 125, 127 top, 142–143, 155, 165 top, 188, 190, 193, 196 top, 196 bottom, 197, 198. © Getty Images / p. 27: Chris Hellier/ Corbis via Getty Images; p. 32 right: E. Bacon/Topical Press Agency/Hulton Archive; p. 33 top: Keystone-France/ Gamma-Keystone; p. 33 bottom: George Rinhart/Corbis; p. 35: George Rinhart/Corbis; p. 40 top: George Rinhart/ Corbis; p. 40 bottom: Topical Press Agency; p. 41: Central Press/Hulton Archive; p. 45 bottom: Patrick Smith; p. 59: Jean MAINBOURG/Gamma-Rapho; p. 64–65: Mike Maloney/ Mirrorpix; p. 67: Walter Looss Jr./Sports Illustrated; p. 70 top: Central Press/ Hulton Archive; p. 71: Lane Stewart/Sports Illustrated; p. 72: Universal/Corbis/VCG; p. 73 top: Reg Lancaster/Daily Express/ Hulton Archive; p. 73 bottom: Rob Taggart/ Central Press; p. 75: Alain MINGAM/ Gamma-Rapho; p. 92: Simon Bruty/ Any Chance; p. 102: Jeff Gross; p. 103: Jeff Gross; p. 122 bottom: Manuel Blondeau/AOP.Press/Corbis; p. 123: Manuel Blondeau/AOP.Press/Corbis; p. 127 bottom: Clive Brunskill; p. 129: Clive Brunskill; p. 136–137: Matthew Stockman; p. 144–145: Ryan Pierse; p. 153: Matthew Stockman; p. 156–157: Jonathan DiMaggio; p. 160: Nick Laham; p. 168: Al Bello; p. 171: Daniel Kopatsch; p. 192: Lintao Zhang; p. 204 top: Jean Catuffe; p. 207 top: Jason Heidrich/ Icon Sportswire; p. 211: Michael Regan; p. 212 top: Scott Heavey; p. 212 bottom: Christopher Lee; p. 216: Oscar J. Barroso/Europa Press; p. 217 left: Fabrizio Carabelli/SOPA Images/ LightRocket. © Presse Sports / p. 130.

Captions

Cover: Suzanne Lenglen, 1926. Rafael Nadal, Roland-Garros, 2008.

Pages 6–7: Babolat, official partner of Roland-Garros, 2011–2019.

Editorial: Virginie Mahieux and Pauline Dubuisson

Graphic design: Elisabeth Welter

Texts: Charlotte Gabas

Image Management : Laetitia Réal-Moretto

Translation from French: Wendy Sweetser

Proofreading: Rachel Zerner

Editorial Partnership : Corinne Schmidt and Charlotte Court

10 9 8 7 6 5 4 3 2 1 Abrams books are available at special discounts when purchased in quantity for premiums and promotions as well as fundraising or educational use. Special editions can also be created to specification.

For details, contact specialsales@abramsbooks.com or the address below.

Abrams® is registered trademark of Harry N. Abrams

Engraving: Verona Libri
Printed and bound in March 2025 by Verona Libri in Italy
Legal deposit: May 2025
ISBN: 978-1-4197-8262-6

US$45 / CAN$57 / UK£35 / €40

ISBN 978-1-4197-8262-6